MUSIC LESSONS
YOU CAN TEACH

MUSIC LESSONS YOU CAN TEACH

Jane L. Reynolds

PARKER PUBLISHING COMPANY, INC.

WEST NYACK, N.Y.

PEP Books Edition . . . . . March 1980

For the teachers and children

HOW THIS BOOK CAN HELP YOU

Can a classroom teacher with little or no music training teach music? What about the person who feels naturally limited because he thinks he cannot "carry" a tune or dance a polka or recognize the tones of a French horn when he hears them? And how should the teacher who has had a great deal of training in music present it in class?

This book has been written for everyone—from the musically skilled to the musically untutored—who will be teaching music in the elementary school. For the music teacher or the person experienced in music, it may serve as a reference book with which to locate quickly such items as: the music and directions for a dance from a foreign country, chords for familiar songs, titles of records that could be used for marching, skipping, and other basic rhythms, information about instruments of the orchestra, etc.

Music Lessons You Can Teach will give the person who feels uncertain about his ability to teach music literally hundreds of lesson ideas. For instance, those who have never approached a musical instrument will find it possible to play piano or Autoharp accompaniments with little or no practice when they follow the suggestions in the chapter on accompanying. Those who have been unsure about the meaning of music symbols may refer to the chapter on music reading. The chapter on music listening gives specific instruction in what the teacher should have students listen for. Exact songs to be used in the classroom are not given, for choice will depend on what music books a school owns. But this book does suggest how the teacher can organize an effective music program by outlining plans on a monthly basis.

As a music teacher of many years' experience, I hold in high regard the classroom teachers on whom I have had to rely to carry on the bulk of the work of music teaching. My primary job has always been, it seems to me, to help classroom teachers discover what they can do with their classes in music. My sincere hope is that this book will help you discover what you can do.

Jane L. Reynolds

USING THIS BOOK

Effective music teaching in the elementary grades starts with long-range planning which provides for experiences in singing, moving in rhythm, playing instruments, reading music, and listening. The materials needed—music books, records, a record player, piano or Autoharp—are items which most schools already have.

Planning by the Month

In some schools the music teacher or consultant makes the plans; in others, the work of planning is left to the classroom teacher. I strongly recommend that every elementary teacher have monthly music outlines so that no area of study is neglected and so that every week or two the children are instructed in at least one area—dancing, reading music, listening—other than singing. From monthly plans it is an easy matter to make daily plans. Outlines made one year can be used other years.

Here is one way to do it. Suppose you are planning for a month that has four weeks of school. Every week you would teach one or two songs chosen from the song books in your classroom. When selecting these you would consider the season of the year, the special days of the month, etc. (A list of special features of the months begins on page 10.) In the first week you might present one of the basic rhythms, in the second teach a dance, during the third study instruments of the orchestra, and in the fourth teach children to listen to a musical masterpiece.

Sample Primary Grade Outline

SEPTEMBER   GRADE 2

Songs: 1. "America"—p. 129 of this book
                  2. "Row, Row, Row Your Boat"—p. 116 of this book

                3.–8. Songs chosen from the children's textbooks.
                      (See suggestions below for subject matter.)
Basic rhythm: Walking—p. 26 of this book
Singing game: "Looby Loo"—p. 46 of this book
Music reading: "Feeling and Hearing Differences in Rhythm"—p. 89 of
                    this book
Listening: "Badinerie" by Bach—p. 163 of this book

Sample Intermediate Grade Outline

SEPTEMBER   GRADE 5

Songs: 1.–6. Songs chosen from the children's textbooks
                      (See suggestions below for subject matter.)
Songs with Autoharp or piano:
                    1. "The More We Get Together"—p. 121 of this book
                    2. "Polly Wolly Doodle"—p. 121 of this book
Dance: "Pop! Goes the Weasel"—p. 59 of this book
Study of percussion instruments: See p. 143 of this book
Listening: "Cat's Fugue" by Scarlatti—p. 174 of this book

Special Days and Features of the Months

SEPTEMBER: Harvest time
             Start of school, school friendships, etc.
             Walking to school, riding the school bus
             Beginning of autumn, cooler weather, hiking
OCTOBER: Fire Prevention Week (early October)
             Columbus Day—October 12
             U.N. Day—October 24
             Halloween—October 31
             Leaves changing colors and falling
NOVEMBER: Veteran's Day—November 11
             Thanksgiving Day—fourth Thursday in November
             Cold weather, need for warmer clothing
DECEMBER: Beginning of winter, first snowfalls
             Hanukkah—date variable
             Christmas—December 25
             New Year's Day—January 1
             Giving and receiving toys and presents
JANUARY: Snow storms, ice and icicles
             Sliding, skating, skiing, etc.
             Building snow forts, making snowmen, etc.
FEBRUARY: Abraham Lincoln's birthday—February 12
             Negro History Week—second week in February
             Valentine's Day—February 14

	George Washington's birthday—February 22
MARCH:	High winds, kite flying
	Saint Patrick's Day—March 17
	Beginning of spring, first flowers, birds return
	Melting ice, flowing brooks, muddy land
	Easter—date variable
APRIL:	All Fool's Day—April 1
	April showers, start of gardening
	Jumping rope, playing marbles, etc.
MAY:	May Day—May 1
	Music Week—first full week of May
	Flowers, green grass, leaves on trees
	Mother's Day—second Sunday in May
	Memorial Day—May 30
JUNE:	Boating, swimming, etc.
	Father's Day—second Sunday in June
	Flag Day—June 14
	Beginning of summer, vacation time
	School graduations

Time Allotments

In grades one, two and three, 20 to 25 minutes a day should be devoted to music. In grades four, five and six, 25 to 30 minutes a day is recommended.

School Programs

Classroom or whole school programs could be developed from the lessons suggested in this book. A few ideas are provided here; as you use the book, you may think of others.

1. A RHYTHMS PROGRAM (Use Chapter 1)

This program could be presented indoors or out and could be done by one or several classes. One group would march to music, another skip, still another gallop, etc. There could be a group to jump rope and another to present a routine with beachballs. Recordings would be used as suggested in Chapter 1.

2. A FOLK DANCE FESTIVAL (Use Chapter 2)

If this program were given out-of-doors, sound amplification would probably be needed. A tape recording of the songs could be made by the children ahead of time and played over a loud speaker. Or, children could take turns being singers and dancers.

Costumes could be simple, or they could be as elaborately authentic

as you wish. A simple "costume" might be bright-colored bow ties for the
boys and colored hair bows for the girls. Both could wear colorful crêpe
paper sashes or wide cummerbunds.

If giving the program out-of-doors, be sure to have at least one alternate
date to provide for inclement weather.

3. A COMMUNITY SING WITH AUTOHARPS (Use Chapter 4)

If your school has two or more Autoharps, they may be used to accompany community singing. Older children may take turns accompanying
songs for which they have learned chord changes beforehand.

You should have enough Autoharps. One instrument for every 20 to
30 people is a good proportion, so, if there are a hundred people singing,
four or more Autoharps will be needed. Words can be shown on a screen by
an overhead projector, and children can take turns pointing to the words
as songs are sung.

If parents are in the audience, they could be asked to sing certain songs
or stanzas of songs alone. The children would sing others alone, but for the
most part, everyone would sing together.

4. THE INSTRUMENTS OF THE ORCHESTRA (Use Chapter 5)

Part One of this program could be a demonstration of how the different types of orchestral instruments were discovered. A rhythm band could
illustrate the beginnings of percussion instruments; Autoharp players could
demonstrate the origin of stringed instruments; players on tuned bottles of
water could show how wind is used both for woodwind and brass instruments,
etc.

In Part Two, children who have had lessons on orchestral instruments
in the various groups could present short selections to demonstrate the tone
of their instruments.

Members of the community who play various instruments well might
end the program with more difficult selections which would demonstrate
the versatility of orchestral instruments.

5. FAMOUS COMPOSERS AND THEIR MUSIC (Use Chapter 6)

For this program, short skits could be written about the lives of three
or more famous composers. Following these presentations, recordings of
some of their shorter compositions could be played, and, if appropriate, the
music could be interpreted through dance. Songs by the composers could
be located and sung.

6. AN OUTDOOR MUSIC FESTIVAL (Use Chapters 1, 2, 4, and 6)

Let me describe one such program which was presented out-of-doors
by a school with about a 150 children in kindergarten through third grade.

The audience was requested to bring their own lawn or folding chairs which they were directed to place around a blacktop area of the playground which was to serve as the stage. Both a record player and a tape recorder were used.

The entrance of classes was to music to which they did basic rhythms. Kindergarteners walked, first graders marched, second graders skipped, and third graders did a step-slide. During the program, kindergarteners performed a simple singing game; first graders played rhythm band instruments and did the Maypole Streamer Dance described on page 47; some second graders jumped rope to music of Vivaldi, others portrayed some of the animals in Saint-Saëns' "Carnival of the Animals"; third graders did a folk dance and a colorful beachball routine. Each grade sang one song accompanied by tape recorder on which piano accompaniment had been taped, and all classes sang "The Happy Wanderer" as everyone marched back into school in time with the music.

Equipment and Supplies

The appendix contains names and addresses of companies that can supply you with the materials you will need.

RECORD PLAYER

Every school should own at least one record player of superior quality, one which will reproduce recordings in the way they were meant to be heard. We would not think of asking children to read or view anything in a room which was dimly lighted. We should have the same standards when we ask them to listen to music. When a listener finds it difficult to discriminate between such instruments as a flute and an oboe, a trumpet and a French horn, a clarinet and a bassoon, it is usually the record player which is defective.

If your school operates on a limited budget and needs to purchase record players, it would be better to buy one quality instrument rather than a number of inferior machines. It should be portable and kept in a place accessible to all classrooms. Ideally every schoolroom would be equipped with a good three-speed record player which has a speaker at least five or six inches in diameter.

A record player is a much-used piece of equipment. You will use it for teaching rhythms, songs, dances, recognizing instruments of the orchestra, music appreciation, etc. You might use it to play story records or, on occasion, play music as a background for study. Any item that is to receive this much use should be sturdily built. If you paid twice as much for a better record player as you would for a cheap one, not only might you get twice the wear in years of use, but also twice the value in quality of sound.

Take good care of your record player. Keep it covered when not in use so that dust cannot get into the mechanism. Watch the stylus (needle).

No stylus is made to last forever, but some are made of more durable material than others. A good one might last a year, poorer ones less. If you begin to notice that records sound "fuzzy" or that the appearance of the grooves on records changes as they are played, consider replacing the stylus.

PIANO

If you plan to use the chapter in this book which tells you how to accompany singing, you will need either a piano or an Autoharp. If your classroom has an old piano, it may serve the purpose, unless it is impossible to tune or is missing strings, keys, hammers, etc. Then it should be discarded. However, just because a piano is old is no reason to have it destroyed. If the tone is good, an unsightly old upright is often to be preferred to a handsome new spinet. If you are offered a used upright for the taking or even for a few dollars, consider appropriating it. However, you should have a piano tuner or other qualified person check the mechanism and general condition to make sure it would be worth acquiring.

Any school interested in purchasing a new piano for a classroom should consider a studio upright, a piano with both good tone and good looks. Spinets are nice looking, but too often the tone is inferior because there is not enough space inside them for long strings and a large sized sounding board.

AUTOHARP

The ideal school has a grand piano in its auditorium and upright pianos in its classrooms. But, if your school budget does not allow the ideal, try an Autoharp. As the name implies, this is an "automatic harp," and it can be played immediately by anyone. It has a pleasing tone and is both portable and durable. A new one can be purchased for around 30 or 40 dollars.

PITCHPIPE

If you do not have a piano or other instrument for starting songs on pitch, you should purchase a pitchpipe.

BOOKS

Most school rooms for grades two through six have sets of song books for the children and teachers' music books in first grade. Many excellent music books are put out by various publishers, and your classroom should have at least one set.

RECORDS

Certain records will be required for presenting the lessons in chapters 1, 5, and 6. Many schools will already own a number of the records suggested.

These were intentionally chosen from standard collections so that purchases would not be costly and could be kept to a minimum.

Results of Using This Book

This book can help classroom teachers bring music to children. Its contents are timely now and can remain timely for as long as people want to dance or to sing songs, for as long as they need to know the meaning of music symbols in order to read music, for as long as they would like to listen intelligently to the music of master composers.

Above all, it is hoped that this book will give you, the classroom teacher, ideas for music lessons which you can present to your classes, and, that by presenting them successfully, you will generate confidence in yourself—confidence that you *do* have the ability to teach music and to teach it well.

Jane L. Reynolds

CONTENTS

13

Chapter 2: You Can Teach Singing Games and Dances (cont.)

Part II: TEACHING SINGING

Chapter 3: You Can Teach Music Reading

Chapter 4: You Can Teach Songs with Accompaniment

Part III: TEACHING MUSIC APPRECIATION

Chapter 5: You Can Teach Recognition of Instruments

MUSIC LESSONS
YOU CAN TEACH

Part One

TEACHING RHYTHMS

Rhythm is inherent in the functioning of the universe. As inhabitants of the planet earth, we are accustomed to such rhythms as one year following another, one season giving way to the next, day following night. Without rhythmic systems, there would be no life.

What is meant by rhythm? Primarily it means the systematic repetition of things or their recurrence in a pattern. It has come to include the rate of speed or tempo at which things move. In music we think of the duration of notes as part of the rhythm.

Human Rhythms

As human beings we expect that events will occur rhythmically, and we are understandably upset when life rhythms are altered. Our bodies pulse in rhythm; hearts beat at a particular rate of speed. In breathing, the inhaling of air is followed by exhaling for as long as we live. In walking, one step counters another, back and forth. Even the two sides of our bodies show repetition, one side fairly well duplicating the other.

Man lives in a daily rhythm of motion and rest. In children's lives there is play and rest; in adult lives, work and rest.

Changes in tempos can be causes for alarm. Up to a point, a heart which beats slightly fast gives a pleasurable sensation; one that is slowed during sleep does no harm. But beyond a certain point, tempo changes can be dangerous to human life. It is not surprising that people resist irregular rhythms.

19

People interrelate in rhythm. The baseball player at bat must sense as the ball is pitched at what precise moment he should swing his bat. Conversations between people have rhythm, even when one person talks twice as much as the other. If an interpersonal relationship is good, the conversation will bounce back and forth like a ping pong ball going from player to player, each person sensing when to speak. People who do not get along well with others usually have rhythms that do not dovetail with the rhythms of those other people.

The Rhythms of Musical Compositions

Musical compositions borrow their rhythm ideas from the rhythms of life. A march rhythm imitates feet walking; a barcarole rhythm imitates the sounds of a boat rocking back and forth in water; a lullaby rhythm imitates slow breathing.

Because music's rhythms are imitations of the rhythms of life, human beings are very sensitive to them. Some time when you are either consciously listening to music or when music is being played near you, think of your breathing. It may surprise you to find that your inhalings are coinciding with strong beats in the music. I have often observed this phenomenon in people seated near me in a concert hall. While some might be obviously swinging a foot or a leg or bobbing their heads in time with the strong beats in the music, every person would in some way be breathing with it, adjusting his breathing when the tempos changed.

The notes of a musical composition follow each other either in a pattern of steady, even beats or in a fast-slow or slow-fast combination. In any succession of notes is an underlying beat which is either sounded or implicit. These beats group into combinations of twos, threes, fours, etc., to form measures. The number of beats in every measure is written at the beginning of the music and is called the time signature. There is always a fraction— 2/4, 3/4, 4/4, 6/8, etc. The top number indicates the grouping or how many beats there are in each measure. The bottom number—usually 2, 4 or 8—indicates the type of note which is given one beat. The number 2 stands for the half note, 4 for the quarter note, 8 for the eighth note.

Rhythmic Divisions in Music

Like sentences with commas and periods and word groupings where the reader takes a breath, musical compositions have stopping or resting places. These are usually evenly spaced, each being a certain number of measures long, and are called phrases.

To see what is meant by the term, let us find the stopping places or ends of phrases in a familiar song. In "Twinkle, Twinkle, Little Star," for instance, we find that the music moves steadily until it stops on the word "star." It then proceeds evenly through ". . . what you are." Continuing thus to the end of the song, we would discover six phrases in all, each having two measures.

Part of responding to the rhythm of music involves hearing phrase divisions. Dances require changes of steps at the ends of phrases, and the lessons in basic rhythms sometimes ask that the performer mark the ends of phrases by changing direction or even by stopping altogether.

Rhythm in Music as a Psychological Factor

Some music irritates us without our knowing why. While the annoyance might be due to the intensity of the sound, the tone of the instruments, or harmonies that we find unpleasant, usually it is the rhythm which is the most bothersome. People who are energetic naturally prefer fast tempos, while slow-moving people prefer slow tempos. Since music compels us to move with it involuntarily in our breathing, etc., being forced to move in time with alien beats can be very annoying.

Every teacher will occasionally find children who apparently cannot consciously keep step with music, not even with a powerful-sounding march. This inability is often noticeable in certain types of disturbed children. Not only will they be unaware of the rhythm of the music; they will also be heedless and inconsiderate of other people. One can postulate that such children are indicating that they feel that other people have no interest in them. They probably find it difficult to trust anyone.

The inability to perform consciously in time with music does not always carry over to listening periods. Troubled children will often listen more attentively to music than will their mentally healthier schoolmates. Perhaps they realize that, in music, rhythm is constant, something to trust and count on. Training in rhythmic response to music is beneficial for all children, but it is especially important for the insecure child.

Rhythm in Music as a Disciplinary Force

We live in an environment that naturally restrains us. We are kept in check by other people, by weather, by innumerable factors. People moving to music's rhythms are also limited, limited in what manner they move, when, and how much. So, if we train children to move rhythmically to music, we will be training them to accept discipline. The person who has a sense of rhythm, who can sing, march, dance, or play an instrument without breaking the rhythm pattern or changing the tempo, is disciplined in a way that is needed when coping with life.

Training Children to Move in Rhythm with Music

Where do we start when we want to train children to respond rhythmically to music? Basic rhythms like walking, marching, running, and the like, are relatively uncomplicated and can usually be performed by the youngest children without any trouble. If children do have difficulty making their feet stay with the music, they should stop and make their hands clap what their feet should be doing. Then they should transfer what they were doing with their hands back to their feet.

The teacher who enjoys dancing will probably want to stress this aspect of music study. Dance is the ultimate in rhythmical response, an ancient pleasure-giving activity which utilizes and combines basic rhythms with various other body motions.

Every class in the elementary school should have training in moving in rhythm with music. How much time is devoted to this study depends on the needs of each class. Maladjusted children would undoubtedly benefit, and all children will enjoy rhythms.

Chapter 1

YOU CAN TEACH BASIC RHYTHMS

Walking is a basic motion that is usually done in rhythm. That is, a regular rate of speed is set and adhered to as one walks. It can be called a basic rhythm. In the same sense, running, skipping, galloping, marching, and any body motion that is done in a similar manner again and again are all basic rhythms.

There are many ways of moving the body rhythmically, and only a few are suggested here. To extend this series of lessons, you could find music for such activities as swaying, pushing and pulling, walking tip-toe, trotting, step-sliding and the like.

Positioning Children for Basic Rhythms

If rhythms are to be done in a classroom which has desks and other furniture, you may ask the children to make a large circle around the edge of the room. Another possibility is to line them up behind a leader, spacing themselves at about arm's length from one another. If the activities are to be done in a room with plenty of space, the children may be allowed to move about freely, as long as they do not bump into one another. When they are to move fast—running, skipping, and the like—children will have less control over their bodies. To prevent accidents, you should choose the direction in which they all should move.

Starting and Stopping Activities

Basic rhythms are performed to music, and it is the music which tells the performers when to start and at what rate of speed to move. If the music

23

has an introduction, the children should not start until it is over. If there is no introduction, you may signal the children to start.

The music also tells performers when to stop. Children doing basic rhythms should be asked to listen carefully for the approaching ending. If they miss it the first time they hear the music, expect them to be ready for it the next time. Sometimes you will have reason to stop the activity before the entire record is over. The best way to do this is to gradually soften the volume of the record player and then remove the needle. As soon as possible after the music has stopped, everyone should be standing still with good spacing between him and the person ahead of him.

Teaching Basic Rhythms with This Book

The following lessons can be used most effectively with young children, although classes of older children could also benefit from performing basic rhythms in time with music. To help you present the lessons, words are suggested. These, however, are merely suggestions and it is hoped that you will motivate, review, and supplement the lessons when needed.

Records

To indicate the sources of records, letters and Roman numerals appear in parentheses after titles. (I, II, III, etc.) are used for grade or album numbers. (R) means the record is in an RCA Victor "Rhythmic Activities" album. (L) stands for RCA Victor "Listening Activities." (AIM) records are in the "Adventures in Music" series, and (BOL) stands for Bowmar Orchestral Library.

THE RHYTHMS

Hand Clapping and Knee Slapping

Preparation for First and Second Lessons

Have ready one or more of the following records: Schumann: "Jaglied" (R I); Burgmuller: "L'Arabesque" (R II); Bach-MacDowell: "March" (R III); Tchaikowsky: "March of the Tin Soldiers" (R III).

First Lesson[1]

Listen to the music on this record. As soon as you know how fast it goes, clap your hands in time with it. Stop when the music stops.

(Play enough of the record to give the children a chance to respond. Then turn down the volume and stop the record.)

---

[1] For ease of reference, throughout the book the teacher's words to the class are enclosed by rules. Instructions to the teacher and answers to questions the teacher asks the class appear in parentheses.

The music that we heard has a steady beat. Some of those beats are stronger than others. When you listen to the music again, decide where the strong beats are. Do you hear LOUD-soft, LOUD-soft, or do you hear LOUD-soft-soft-soft, LOUD-soft-soft-soft? When I signal, clap what you are hearing.

———————————————

(Play the record. After a few moments, signal to the children to clap as suggested.)

———————————————

Every time you clapped a set of loud and soft beats, you clapped a measure of music. This time when you respond to the music, slap your knees on the strong beats and clap your hands lightly on the weak ones.

———————————————

(Play the record. If the children have difficulty coordinating the motions, signal them to stop and help them start again on one of the accented beats.)

Second Lesson

———————————————

The last time we listened to a rhythm record, we slapped our knees on the strong beats and clapped our hands on the weak ones.

———————————————

(If the children had difficulty at the previous lesson, the activity may be reviewed.)

———————————————

What do we call each group of loud and soft beats in music? (A measure) Notes are grouped in measures, and measures fall naturally into groups. Did you ever notice how music moves along for a while, slows down or stops, and then starts up again? It is what people do when they talk. Every so often they slow down or stop, usually to take a breath. Music has breathing places, too, and these pauses show the beginning and end of phrases.

Today we are going to listen for the pauses in the music which mark the ends of phrases. The moment one phrase ends, another one starts. Usually it happens very quickly, so when you hear the music coming to one of those stopping places, raise your hand very briefly.

———————————————

(Play the record. While it is relatively easy to find phrases in songs, it is not as easy in instrumental music. Remember that there will only be two or four or maybe eight measures in each phrase.)

———————————————

You have learned to hear beats in music and to recognize measures with strong and weak beats. You can also find phrases. We will divide into two groups. (Assign one half of the children to Group One, the others to Group Two.) Group One will start and Group Two will listen. For the first phrase Group One will slap knees and clap hands. They will stop and Group Two will slap and clap the second phrase. Continue to take turns until the music ends.

(Play the record. Direct the groups if necessary.)

Preparation for Third Lesson

Have ready a record in 3/4 time: Brahms: "Waltz No. 1" (R II); English: "Lavender's Blue" (R III).

Third Lesson

When we listen to music and hear the beats go LOUD-soft, LOUD-soft, we know that there are two beats in every measure. When we hear LOUD-soft-soft-soft, LOUD-soft-soft-soft, how many beats are there in every measure? (Four) As you listen to this new record, count the beats in every measure. Do not clap.

(Play the record for a few moments, lower volume and stop.)

How many beats did you hear in the measures? (Three)

When people march or dance or move in time with music, they must be able to hear the loud and soft beats in every measure, and they must be able to hear phrases begin and end.

We will listen to the whole record this time. During the first phrase, you will clap the beats with your hands—LOUD-soft-soft, LOUD-soft-soft. When you hear the music change to the second phrase, slap your knees in the same way. On the third phrase, clap hands again, and keep going, alternating every phrase.

(Play the record. Most phrases in 3/4 time will be four measures long. If necessary, help children who have difficulty.)

Walking

Preparation for Lessons

Have ready one or more of the following records: Jadassohn: "Air de Ballet" (R II); Old Hunting Song: "John Peel" (R III); Grainger: "Country Gardens" (R VI).

First Lesson

We can make our feet move in many different ways. We can make them run or gallop or hop. What else can we make them do? (Walk, march, skip, jump, slide, skate, etc.)

As you listen to this record, think what the music tells your feet to do. Don't do it yet.

——————————————

(Play the record for a few moments, lower volume and stop.)

——————————————

What do you think the music told your feet to do? (Walk)

——————————————

(Position the children for walking. They can either line up behind a leader at arm's length from each other, or make a circle, drop hands, and face in one direction.)

——————————————

Stand still in your places. When the music starts, clap every beat in the way that your feet should walk. When I signal, start to walk with the music. Drop your hands to your sides and let your arms swing freely. Stop when the music stops.

——————————————

(Play the record. When everyone is clapping the beats correctly, signal them to stop clapping and start walking.)

Second Lesson

——————————————

As soon as you know what this music tells your feet to do, raise your hands. Remember, don't do it yet.

——————————————

(For a few moments, play either the record used in the first lesson or a different one for walking. Lower the volume and stop.)

——————————————

What did the music tell your feet to do? (Walk)

Imagine that you are taking a walk to somewhere special. Where might you go? (To the store, through the woods, along the seashore, etc.) What might you see as you walk along? (People, automobiles, buildings, birds, gardens, airplanes, etc.) As you are walking, what else might you do? (Look in the trees for birds, stop to talk to people, buy something inside a store, stop before crossing a street, etc.)

Today when you walk to the music, pretend that you are walking somewhere in particular. It could be somewhere we just suggested or a place of your own choosing. Perhaps you will stop walking for a moment. If you do and you then start again, remember to make your feet keep time with the music. See if I can guess by watching you what it was you were doing on your walk.

——————————————

(Play the record. If it is a short composition, you may need to play it more than once.)

——————————————

Return to your seats. Raise your hands if you want to tell us where you imagined you went and what you imagined you did.

Marching

Preparation for Lessons

Have ready at least one of the following records: Pinto: "March, Little Soldier" (L I); Pierne: "March of the Little Lead Soldiers" (L I, BOL #54); Elgar: "Pomp and Circumstance No. 1" (BOL #54); Herbert: "March of the Toys" (AIM II); Sousa: "Semper Fidelis" (AIM III, Vol. 2); Sousa: The Stars and Stripes Forever" (AIM IV, Vol. 2; BOL #54).

First Lesson

The music you will hear today will tell your feet to walk in a special way. Raise your hands if you know what it is.

(Play the record for a few moments, lower volume and stop.)

What would feet do to that music? (March) When several people march together in formation, what do we call it? (A parade) How is marching different from walking? (People keep their backs straight, arms at their sides, and eyes looking straight ahead. They raise their knees high as they move.)

(Position the children for marching. If they line up behind a leader, they should be at arm's length from each other. If they make a circle, they should all face in the same direction.)

When you are ready to march, your backs will be straight, your arms will be by your sides, and your eyes will be looking straight ahead of you. Wait until I signal you to start marching. (Tell the children what the signal will be—a clap of the hands, "Forward, march!" the start of the leader, etc.)

(Play the record. If the march has an introduction, your signal to start will come at the end of this passage. The children may tire of marching if the music lasts too long, in which case you should turn down the volume and stop the record.)

Second Lesson

Today we will hear the music for marching once again. Take the places you had last time. Show how you will keep your backs, where your arms will be, and where your eyes will look.

(When the children are ready, start the record, and give them the signal to start. If the record is not finished at the end of a minute or two, lower the volume and stop.)

When people are in a parade, they do not always move ahead. Sometimes they must wait in one place for one reason or another. If the music is still playing, the parade leader might shout: "Mark time!" Then the marchers would keep their feet moving without going anywhere. Try that now. I will signal you to start and stop. Ready. One-two-mark-time-one-two-one-two . . . .

(Expect the children to mark time without music at the speed suggested by your voice until you tell them to stop.)

Have you ever noticed how similar people look when they are in a parade? Their uniforms are the same or similar. They have the same straight posture; they face in the same direction. As they march, they all step on the same foot at the same time. Do you know which foot is used to start marching? (Left) Everyone in a parade steps on his left foot when he hears a strong beat.

Listen to the music again. When you are sure which are the strong beats, say the word "LEFT" for these and "right" for the others. Then mark time as you say "LEFT-right-LEFT-right." When I signal, stop chanting and march forward.

(Play the record. The children will chant "LEFT-right" and mark time. When all are doing this correctly, signal them to march forward with a hand clap or the words, "Forward, march," or whatever signal you choose. After they have marched for a while, signal the children to mark time again. Check to see that everyone is still stepping on his left foot for the strong beats.)

Third Lesson

The music for marching which we heard in past lessons had more than one tune. Sometimes we heard the same tune played over again. Today as you listen to the music, try to hear these tunes when they start. Wait until one tune has finished and then raise your hands when you think a tune is starting.

(If it is not too long, play the record all the way through. Usually the first tune is repeated, and hands should be raised at the beginning of this repeat. Children should not raise their hands for every phrase, only for the beginning of themes.)

———————

Take your places for marching.

When you march today, march forward while the first tune is playing. Then turn about and march in the opposite direction during the next part of the music. Every time you hear a change and a tune begins, turn and march in the other direction.

Let's practice making turns before we do it with music. Mark time, LEFT-right-LEFT-right. Now, forward, march . . . About face and forward, march. . . About face and forward, march. (Practice until the children make turns smoothly.)

Remember when the music plays that you should turn at exactly the moment one tune ends and the next one begins.

———————

(Play the record. Everyone should start marching with his left foot first. If they listen carefully, the children should be able to "about face" when the music "tells" them to.)

Skipping

Preparation for Lessons

Have ready one or more of the following records: Corelli: "Gigue in A" (R I); Balfe: "Happy and Light of Heart" (R II); Mendelssohn: "Tarantelle" (R II); Corelli: "Gigue in B♭" (R IV).

First Lesson

———————

The music we are going to hear today is a little too fast for walking. It isn't good for marching either. As you listen to the record, try to decide what feet might do to it.

———————

(Play the record a few moments, lower the volume and stop.)

———————

What do you think that music tells feet to do? (Let the children answer. They heard music for skipping, but this music sounds very similar to music for galloping. Any child who suggests that it is galloping music should be told that he has given a "good answer." The notes of a gallop are usually even— ♪♪♪ ♪♪♪ while those for skipping are usually more uneven— ♩ ♪♩ ♪ .)

To skip with music, we must have a lot of space ahead of us. Make as wide a circle as possible around the outside of the room. Drop hands, and make sure there is a good space between yourself and the next persons. Turn in the direction I point. (Indicate a direction for all to face.)

One of the tricks of good skipping is to try to push yourself high in the air. The first time you come down, one foot will be ahead; the next time, the other foot will lead, back and forth. You make little extra hops as part of your skip.

(Play the record. If there are children who are having difficulty, ask the good skippers to take them in hand to help them.)

The best way to become a good skipper is to practice when you have time. Skip in your play area at home. Skip on the playground at school. Rest a moment now, and then we will practice again. Be sure there is plenty of space ahead of you.

(Play the record again. If the children become tired, lower the volume and stop the record.)

Second Lesson

Today we will hear again the music for skipping. As you listen, try to remember how the first tune sounds at the beginning. If you hear it start again, raise your hands. If you hear another tune, raise your hands. In other words, raise your hands at the beginning of every tune.

(Play the record. The children should wait until a tune is finished before they raise their hands for the next one. Tunes will probably be two phrases long.)

We will be divided into two groups and will take turns skipping. Only the children in Group One will skip while the first tune plays the first time. They will stop and Group Two will take a turn skipping to the tune that follows. They will stop and Group One will skip again, and so forth.

(Divide the class. Where the groups are positioned will depend on the amount of space available and on the visual pattern you want to effect. In a large room, groups could take corners diagonally opposite each other, facing. When the music starts, the first group would skip across the intervening space, turn around and wait. When the next tune starts, Group Two would skip across, turn and wait. Group One would skip again, and so forth. In a smaller room, both groups could make a line with Group One in the lead. When the music starts, Group One would skip forward and would stop without turning when the tune ended. Group Two would skip during the next tune, stop and wait, and so forth. When the space for skipping is limited, suggest that everyone skip high, moving forward very little with each skip.)

Galloping

Preparation for the Lessons

Have ready one or more of the following records: English Folk: "Come Lasses and Lads" (R III); Godard: "Postillion" (R III); von Suppé: "Light Cavalry Overture" (L II); Schumann: "The Wild Horseman" (L II); Kullak: "The Little Hunter" (L II).

First Lesson

The music which we shall hear today is something like music for skipping. As you listen to it, decide what it tells your feet to do. Don't do it yet.

(Play the record a few moments, lower the volume and stop.)

What do you think the music tells your feet to do? (Gallop) What is the difference between skipping and galloping? (Skipping is done first with one foot leading and then with the other. Galloping is usually done with just one foot in the lead.) Who will show us how to gallop?

(Invite one or more children to demonstrate galloping.)

Make a large circle around the room. Then drop hands and face in the direction I show you. (Point out the direction.)

When the music begins, start galloping to one side. When you hear a tune start—either the same one or a new one—change feet and gallop to the other side. When you hear a change of tunes again, change sides again.

(Play the record. Galloping is a strenuous activity and can be done only for short periods of time. If the record is long and the children become tired, lower the volume and stop the record.)

Second Lesson

When people are going somewhere, they don't usually gallop. But there are animals that gallop to get places. Can you name any? (Horses, ponies, zebras reindeer, giraffes, etc.)

Let's decide together which animal we will imitate as we gallop to music today. (If it is near Christmas, the children might like to gallop lightly like reindeer. If it is near circus-time or summer, they might choose to gallop proudly like circus horses or ponies. If they are studying animals that might be seen in a zoo, they might prefer to gallop heavily like buffalo or giraffes.)

(If there is enough space, the children can move freely about the room. Play the record.)

Running

Preparation for the Lesson

Have ready one of the following records: Moszkowski: "Sparks" (R I); Kopylow: "Etude Joyeuse" (R I); Glock: "Ballet" (R I); Gurlitt: "Running Game" (R II); Mozart: "Gavotte" (R V).

The Lesson

The music on the record we are to hear will not tell your feet to walk or march or gallop. As you listen, think what it tells you to do. Remember, don't do it yet.

(Play the record for a few moments, lower the volume and stop.)

What did the music tell your feet to do? (Run) Most children like to run when they are playing, especially out-of-doors. They usually run as fast as they wish. But when people run with music, they must listen to the notes and try to make their feet stay with them.

Make a circle around the room, spreading out as much as you can. Then drop hands and face in the direction I point.

After you have listened to the music for a few moments, try to clap with it in the way your feet would run. When everyone's hands are clapping correctly, I will give you a signal to start running. Your feet should go as fast as your hands clapped.

(Play the record. When the children are clapping with the notes, signal them to run.)

We are going to take turns running. There will be two circles, one outside the other. To find out who will be in each one, you will count off by twos. The first child will count "one," the next "two," the next "one," and so on. (Children count off.)

All children who said "one" step to the inside and face left. The "Twos" will be on the outside and will face right.

When the music starts, the inside circle will start running while the outside circle stands still. When the first tune ends, the inside circle will stop and wait while the outside circle runs. On the next tune, it will be the turn of the inside circle. Take turns until the last tune when both circles will move.

_____

(Play the record. It may take a few attempts before everyone can anticipate the last section of the music when the two circles run simultaneously in opposite directions.)

_____

Skating

Preparation for the Lesson

Have ready one of the following records: Poldini: "Valse Serenade" (R I); Czibulka: "Love's Dream After the Ball" (R I); Kullak: "Skating" (R II); Waldteufel: "The Skater's Waltz" (R IV); Meyerbeer: "Waltz" from "Les Patineurs" (AIM II).

The Lesson

_____

Have you ever skated on ice? If you haven't, have you ever seen people skating in movies? When people are wearing skates on ice, they cannot walk or run or do too many of the things they usually do with their feet. Could someone show us how people skate on ice? (Invite at least one child to demonstrate.) Notice how a skater first pushes one foot and then the other out to the side. He keeps his weight on the foot that is not pushing.

_____

(Position the children around the room with space enough for skating.)

_____

The music you will hear is music for skating. Stand still and listen to it for a moment. Then clap the strong beats, the beats you would skate to. Your clapping will be slow. When I signal you, you may start skating.

_____

(Play the record. The children should clap the beat of the foot stroke before trying to "skate." If the record is very long, stop it before the children become tired.)

_____

You will be skating with a partner. (Assign partners or let children choose them, preferably boy-girl.) Pretend there are little ponds of ice in space areas around the room, and go there with your partners. Boys should cross hands, wrist over wrist, and their partners should take both hands. Partners will skate together in the same direction.

_____

(Play the record. The pairs of skaters could circle their imaginary ponds, skate to the next "pond," circle there, go to the next, etc.)

Hopping and Jumping

Preparation for Jumping Lesson

Have ready one of the following records: Gurlitt: "Jumping" (R II); Bergmuller: "La Bergeronette" (R II); Tchaikowsky: "March of the Tin Soldiers" (R III).

Jumping Lesson

What is the difference between hopping and jumping? (Let the children discuss the question.) A hop is done quickly with a little spring. It is so quick and covers such a short distance, people can do it on one foot. A jump is a long leap into the air. It is usually done on both feet.

People don't usually hop or jump when they want to go somewhere, but there are creatures that do. What animals use jumping? (The children should discuss this. Grasshoppers take long jumps, and animals like panthers and leopards jump on occasion. The kangaroo is perhaps the most well-known jumping animal.) What creatures are able to hop? (The children will probably name frogs, rabbits, toads, birds, etc.) As you listen to this music, decide if it is music for hopping or for jumping.

(Play the record for a few moments, lower the volume and stop.)

Pretend you are an animal like the kangaroo which must jump to get around. You look about you until you see something good to eat a little way off. You take a few jumps in that direction, and you stop a moment to eat. You look around again, and you see another place to go. You jump over there for a few moments. This means that some kangaroos will be standing still while others are moving. And when kangaroos move, they will move only as fast as the music is moving.

(Play the record. If it is short and the children have rested between periods of jumping and are not tired, play it again.)

Preparation for Hopping Lesson

Have ready one of the following records: Gounod: "Les Piferari" (R II); Grainger: "Country Gardens" (R VI).

Hopping Lesson

What does this music tell you to do?

(Play enough of the record for the children to identify it as music for hopping. Lower the volume and stop.)

What did the music tell you to do? (Hop) Hopping is a short, quick movement done by small creatures like frogs, toads, rabbits, and birds. Children also like to hop, and sometimes they play hopping games. Can you name one of these games? (Hopscotch is familiar to most children.) When children hop, they usually hop on just one foot at a time.

Make a circle around the room. Then drop hands and face in the direction I show you. (Point out the direction for all to face.) Wait until you have heard the music before you start to hop. I will signal you to start. Hop on one foot while the first tune plays. Change to your other foot for the next tune. Keep changing feet every time a tune begins.

(Play the record. Signal the children to start hopping.)

Jumping with a Jumprope

Preparation for the Lessons

Have on hand one or more of the following records: Corelli: "Gigue in A" (R I); English Folk: "Come Lasses and Lads"; English Folk: "Polly Put the Kettle On" (R III). Jumpropes will be needed at the second lesson.

First Lesson

When people jump rope, they must guess exactly when the rope will swing under their feet. Arms swing and feet jump—swing and jump, swing and jump.

Stand at your places. Pretend you have a jumprope in your hands. You swing it over your head and you jump when your arms swing down. Try it. Swing and jump, swing and jump.

(Children try swinging and jumping without music.)

When we jump rope with music, we must all jump at the same time. We will hear the tapping of the ropes as they all hit the floor together and everyone's feet coming to the floor at the same time. Listen to the record for a few moments until you can feel when to swing and when to jump. I will signal you to start.

(Play the record. After a few measures of listening, signal the children to start swinging and jumping with imaginary ropes.)

At our next lesson, we will jump with real ropes. If you do not have a jumprope from a store, find a piece of old clothesline which will work just as well, and bring it to the next lesson. Practice jumping rope in your spare time.

Preparation for Second and Third Lessons

The children should have the jumpropes which they have brought from home. If everyone is to jump at the same time, the class should be in a large area with a minimum of furniture.

Second Lesson

We need a lot of space when we swing ropes. (Position the children with ample space between them.)

When we jump rope to music, the music will tell us when to jump and will help us stay together. It can also tell us when to change our way of jumping or when to take a rest. If we jump to a tune, we will probably jump eight times. If we rest during a tune, we will rest eight counts. Let's try that—jump to a tune and rest for the next. I will signal you to start.

(Play the record. Signal the children to start after the introduction if there is one, or let them listen to the first tune. Help them take breaks, start again, etc.)

This time we will be divided into two groups and will take turns jumping. (Divide the children into groups.) Group One will jump while the first tune plays, Group Two will jump for the next playing of a tune, then Group One will jump again, and so forth.

(Play the record. Direct the children as little as possible.)

Third Lesson

Go with your jumpropes to the places you had at the last lesson. We will again jump by groups.

(Play the record for a quick review.)

When people jump rope for a long time, they become tired. For this reason, I would like you to think of other ways to swing ropes in rhythm. Put both ends of your jumprope in your right hand. As the music plays, try to find ways of moving your rope with it.

(Play the record. The children's experiments will probably include swinging ropes overhead, to the side, under feet, etc.)

One person will lead us in swinging our jumpropes. (Choose a child who keeps time well and who can hear changes in the tunes. He should stand ahead of the group where he can be seen and with his back to the others.) Group One will jump with the first tune, Group Two with the second. Then put your rope ends in your right hands and swing your ropes as the leader swings his.

(Play the record. This activity may be repeated with different leaders, with additional rope jumping and other variations.)

Beachball Activities

Although bouncing or tossing a ball is not a basic rhythm in the usual sense, it does require coordination and is an activity repeated rhythmically. Also, a beachball routine to music makes a colorful and effective number for an assembly program.

Preparation for the Lessons

Have ready a record in waltz rhythm or one of the following: Schumann: "Papillons No. 8" (R III); English Folk: "Lavender's Blue" (R III); Schubert: "Waltz Op. 9a., No. 3" (R III); Schumann: "March" (R V). For the first lesson, have one large ball. Have a ball for every other child at the second lesson.

First Lesson

When a group of people want to do an activity together, music can help them. When a group wants to bounce balls together, they can play music which tells them exactly when to start, how fast to go, and when to stop.

Stand at your places. Imagine you have a ball. When the music starts, wait four slow counts. Then clap once for every time the ball would touch the floor. One person may bounce and catch the real ball. (If there are more balls, let children use them.)

(If the record is short, play it all the way through. If it is long, play it for a few moments, lower the volume and stop.)

What else could you do in time with music, using a large ball? (Suggestions might be: (1) toss in the air and catch, (2) toss back and forth to another person, (3) bounce back and forth to someone, (4) throw overhand to another. If children suggest rolling it across the floor to someone, explain that it is difficult to control the rate of speed and stay with the music.)

Choose one of the activities you just suggested. (Let the children decide.) This time when the music plays, clap for bouncing until the end of the first tune. Then pretend to do the activity you have chosen for the second tune, bounce again for the next tune, and so forth until the music ends. Two children will do the activities with the ball we have here.

(Play the record. Give help only if needed.)

If you have them at home, bring in large beachballs about the size of basketballs for our next lesson.

Second Lesson

(Ideally there will be one ball for every two children. If possible, have the lesson in an area with a lot of space.)

Today we will work out a routine with our large balls. At our last lesson, most of us did activities without balls. Who remembers what we did last time? (Bounced balls to the first tune, did a second activity to the next tune, bounced again, and so forth.) Let's try those activities today with balls and with partners.

(Play the record.)

Can you think of a third activity that would go well with the two we were doing? (You will want to experiment with a routine, and, if this activity is to be used in a program, you will want to practice and perfect it.) Can we bounce on the first tune, do the first activity chosen on the next, a different activity on the next, and repeat to the end of the record?

(Play the record.)

Chapter 2

YOU CAN TEACH SINGING
GAMES AND DANCES

The music program in the elementary school should include singing games in the primary grades and folk dances in all grades. Dancing is an activity enjoyed by people of any age. It can contribute to one's well-being by providing opportunities for muscle coordination, mental concentration, and healthful exercise. Through dancing, children can learn group cooperation, for it is a means by which they may come in contact with one another in a socially acceptable way.

To dance is to move the body rhythmically through space, usually to an accompaniment of music. Since it is by means of feet and legs that we propel our bodies, we must remember that there are a limited number of ways to accomplish this. We can walk, run, skip, gallop, jump, hop—steps which have previously been referred to as basic rhythms. Folk dances and singing games utilize these steps either singly or in combination, adding various other body motions which will relate the dancer to his partner or to the group.

How and Why Dance Originated

Children, especially those in the intermediate grades, should be asked to contemplate how they think dancing started, because to know why people chose to invent dance is to understand why we enjoy it and how it benefits us.

Dancing starts as a feeling within the creator. In folk dancing, the feeling usually expressed is joy. Before converting his feelings into a dance, the joyous person may have laughed and shouted, clapped his hands, jumped up and down, skipped and twirled himself about. Soon after he had thus expressed himself, the happy feeling may have subsided or even vanished. To prolong the feeling, to keep it alive, he would create a dance.

Joy is the usual motivation for folk dancing, but students should be led to realize that this is not the only feeling which people might wish to express. While suffering from grief or misfortune, an unhappy person might shake his head, wring his hands, or pace the floor. Dances can stem from sad as well as happy feelings.

By means of dancing, the creator can give form and order to emotions. The presence of other participants, either performing or observing, can help intensify feelings when such persons share them in performance or experience them vicariously as an audience.

How Music Helps Dancing

By adding a musical accompaniment, the creator of the dance adds a spur by which people will feel not only inclined to start but also to continue dancing for a period of time. Music has the power to stimulate dancers and to encourage them to persevere. Its rhythm helps them keep together.

The music of a dance can remind people when they hear it of the original feeling that was experienced during the dance. Children can be led to understand how the sounds of dance music can help people recapture the feelings that originally went with the dance.

Teaching Folk Dancing

Every country or society of people has its folk dances. In most of them there is much stamping of feet, skipping, and general cavorting about— usually body motions which one associates with joy. Ask students to think of possible reasons for people to feel thus in their particular area of the world. They should easily imagine the elation of people of farming countries who, having worked hard for a long period of time, have harvested a good crop. They should imagine that, when fishermen of a country like Norway have returned safely home with a good catch, everyone feels like celebrating.

Ask children to guess why people sometimes stamp their feet when they dance. Is it to help keep warm? Is it to show strength? Can they guess why the dance music of Latin America has an invigorating syncopation? One would expect a more lackadaisical music from countries with a hot climate. Does the syncopation act as a stimulus to help dancers keep moving even when they feel hot?

Then children should speculate about the feelings of the peoples whose dance music was written in the joyless minor mode. Were they despondent because the weather was cold and, therefore, living was difficult? Were they discouraged because food was scarce?

After they have learned a few folk dances from European countries, the students may notice that many have similarities in the steps and in the music. Help them to realize that, in the first place, there are only a few ways to move the feet and legs. They should remember that in Europe it is easy to travel among smaller countries that are located close together, and this means that many cultural elements like music and dance steps could be borrowed or exchanged. Also, since climate, terrain, and the occupations of the people are similar, it is likely they would invent similar dances.

Teaching Dances from Other Times

When performing a dance of long ago, students can learn much about the people from hearing the music and doing the dance. The minuet, for example, was a formal dance which was popular during the time of Washington. In those days people were very polite and careful, restricting themselves by their manners. Tight clothing restrained their bodies so that even walking was difficult. Ladies wore fancy wigs, laced bodices, and cumbersome skirts. Men moved stiffly because they wore high collars, ruffles at wrists and neck, pants joined at the knees by stockings, and wigs upon their heads. Because of these hindrances, people could not allow themselves to dance with abandon. When children of today dance the minuet in a slow and deliberate manner, they will learn much about the feelings of people who lived in the eighteenth century.

A Suggested Procedure for Teaching Folk Dances

Following are ideas for the teacher who wishes to enrich the lessons on folk dancing with a study of the peoples and the various factors in their environments which contribute to the creating of dances.

First Lesson

The music of the song which we will learn today is from . . . (country). Later we will learn the dance to it.

(Teach the song.)

The song we have just learned is for dancing. What feeling was expressed in the words and music? (Joy, calmness, sadness, contentment, etc.) Can you guess why the people of this particular country felt this way? (Maybe they wanted to celebrate success in farming, the end of a long period of work, a wedding, an engagement, happiness in being together, a change to good weather, etc.)

Why do you suppose people, any people, create dances? (Possible answers include: so that people can express feelings, to stretch out the enjoyment of feelings, to have pleasant associations with other people, to share enjoyable feelings with others, etc.)

Folk dancing is always done to music. How does music help dancers? (It helps them do their steps together; the rhythm helps people keep going because they want to keep up with it; it expresses the feeling of the people; any time people hear it, it will remind them of the enjoyment they felt when they were dancing, etc.)

Second Lesson

Let's sing by memory the dance song which we learned at a recent lesson. (Review song.)

Today we will learn the dance. (Look in the text beside the word "Formation." If a separate singing group is suggested, proceed as follows.) Because it is difficult to sing and dance at the same time, some of you will sing while the others are dancing. Later, the singers will have a turn at being the dancers. (Choose a group, or suggest that half the children be dancers.)

The dancers will make the formation. (Read the directions under "Formation.")

We will walk through the more difficult steps first. (Read the underlined parts and have the dancers practice them.)

Here are the directions for the first part of the dance. We will walk them through without music. (Children walk through as much as they can do well.) Now we will try the next part. (Continue until all or most of the dance has been attempted.)

We will now try the dance with the music. This time the singers may dance while the dancers sing.

Third Lesson

Today we will review the dance we learned at our last lessons.

As you learn more dances, you will probably notice that many are similar to others. This is especially true when countries are located close to one another; they can easily exchange ideas across the border. Can you think of additional reasons why some dances might resemble others? (Possible reasons might include the fact that there are not too many different steps that people can do in dancing; people whose occupations are alike might think similarly and create dances in a similar manner; if climate and land formations are the same, people might have similar feelings and produce similar dances, etc.)

Some dances are unlike others. Factors in geographical location and the history and development of peoples undoubtedly account for most of these dissimilarities. Can you name some of these factors and suggest the kind of dances that might be created by the people as a result? (A dance from a warm climate might have graceful, easy motions; a vigorous dance might have been created by people living in a cold climate who must keep moving to keep warm; a dance from a country which has bodies of water which freeze in winter might have swaying motions which remind one of skating; a dance from a country which has fought many wars might have forceful motions like foot stamping, etc.)

Think of the steps and the motions you did when you performed the dance we reviewed today, and think of the country from which it came. We have been discussing how factors like geographical location probably contribute to people's thinking when they are making up dances. Can you suggest how the people of this country may have been influenced to create this particular dance?

With these lessons we have not only learned a dance which we can enjoy, but we have learned much about the people who created the dance. By dancing as they have danced, we have been able to feel as they have felt.

Teaching Singing Games and Dances with This Book

This book recommends specific grades in which to present the various games and dances. This does not mean that children of other grades will not be willing or able to perform them. I have seen third graders doing well at square dancing and the Virginia Reel, both of which are recommended for upper grades. It simply takes younger children longer to master the steps and remember the patterns. On the other hand, older children can perform the easier dances, but there is a chance they might become bored or otherwise unhappy with an activity which does not challenge their abilities.

All of the singing games and folk dances in this book are written as songs. Everyone should be familiar with the song before the dance is started. In many cases it is not feasible for the dancers to attempt to sing while they are dancing, and accordingly a separate singing group is suggested under "Formation."

The more difficult steps or motions for each dance are italicized in the text. After the dancers have made the formation, these should be practiced without music. Then the whole dance should be walked through before the music is added.

The number of lessons you present when teaching a dance will depend on such factors as: the amount of time you devote to each lesson, the learning ability of your class, and whether or not you want to perfect the dance for your own satisfaction or for performance in public.

THE GAMES AND DANCES

Bluebird, Bluebird (Grades 1, 2)

Formation

Any number may play this game. Children make a circle, facing center, hands joined. One child is chosen to be the bluebird. The others lift arms to make windows.

Bluebird, Bluebird

Texas Singing Game

Blue - bird, blue - bird, through my win - dow,

Blue - bird, blue - bird, through my win - dow,

Blue - bird, blue - bird, through my win - dow,

Oh, John - ny, aren't you tired?

Take a lit - tle { boy / girl } and tap { him / her } on the shoul - der,

Take a lit - tle { boy / girl } and tap { him / her } on the shoul - der,

Take a lit - tle { boy / girl } and tap { him / her } on the shoul - der,

Oh, John - ny, aren't you tired?

Game

Meas. 1–8   Child who is bluebird "flies" in and out the windows, ending outside circle. Children lower arms.

Meas. 9–14   The "bluebird" stands behind another child and taps him on the shoulders in time with the music.

Meas. 15–16   The child who has been tapped leaves his place and follows the "bluebird" who walks behind the circle.

When the song begins again, the circle of children lifts arms and the second child joins the first in "flying" in and out windows. For measures 9–14, each stands behind another child and taps him on the shoulders so that the third time the song is sung, there will be four bluebirds. The game may be continued for as long as desired.

Looby Loo (Grades 1, 2)

Looby Loo

English Singing Game

First note: F

Piano: L-R

Chords: F, C7

Refrain

Here we go loo - by loo, _____

Here we go loo - by light, _____ Here we go loo - by

loo, _____ All on a Sat - ur - day night. _____ *Fine*

1. You put your right hand in, You

take your right hand out, You give your hand a

shake, shake, shake, And turn your - self a - bout. Oh,

D.C. al Fine

2. You put your left hand in, etc.
3. You put your right foot in, etc.
4. You put your left foot in, etc.
5. You put your head in, etc.
6. You put your whole self in, etc.

Formation

Any number may play this game. Children make a large circle turned clockwise.

Game

Meas. 1–8   *All skip forward. Stop on the words, "Saturday night."*
Meas. 9–16   All face center and do the motions for the stanza.

Maypole Streamer Dance (Grades 1, 2)

Supplies Needed

Packages of colored crepe paper (at least three packages for a class of 25)
Two paper plates about nine inches in diameter
Ruler, scissors, and paste
A window-raising pole or any pole six to seven feet in length

Directions for Making the Maypole

Lay the ruler on the length of the folded package of crepe paper and mark off strips two inches wide. Cut through all thicknesses. Make enough strips to allow one streamer for each child.

Position one end of each strip so that it rests about two inches over the edge of one of the paper plates. The strips will overlap and should be as equidistant from each other as possible. If different colors are used, alternate as desired. Paste the ends onto the plate. Then paste the second plate over the first so that it covers and secures the streamer ends.

Poke a small hole in the exact center of the plates, just large enough to insert the metal end of the window pole, or use one nail to fasten the plates to any other type of pole.

Formation

Choose one child to be the pole holder. Dancers make a circle around the pole and stand about five feet away. The teacher should hand each child a streamer in the order in which the streamers come from the top. Children should be cautioned not to stretch the crepe paper. They should hold them in their right hands.

Dance

Maypole Streamer Dance

J. L. R.

1. Swing and swing and turn a - round,
2. Swing and swing and turn a - round,

Once a - gain, we get un - wound.
Once a - gain, we get un - wound.

To the left we run and then,
To the cen - ter, bend - ing low,

1. To the right, we're back a - gain.

2. Back and high, our stream - ers go.

2. Swing and swing and turn around,
   Once again, we get unwound.
   Skipping left, our streamers high,
   Skipping right on feet that fly.

   Swing and swing and turn around,
   Once again, we get unwound.
   Gallop on a merry chase,
   Gallop right, we're back in place.

STANZA 1, FIRST ENDING

Meas. 1–4   Dancers swing streamers to the left, to the right, and
             hold them raised while turning under counterclock-
             wise.

Meas. 5–8   Repeat the above, making a clockwise turn.

Meas. 9–12   Take ten running steps left and turn (two counts).

Meas. 13–16   Take 12 running steps back to place.

REPEAT, SECOND ENDING

Meas. 1–8   Repeat the swing-swing-turn pattern described above.

Meas. 9–12   Take four slow steps to center, bending low with stream-
               ers.

Meas. 13–16   Take four slow steps backward, raising streamers.

STANZA 2

Do as the words suggest. At the end, dancers let go of their streamers
so that they float to the center.

Shoo, Fly, Don't Bother Me (Grades 1,2,3)

Shoo, Fly, Don't Bother Me

American Singing Game

Formation

Any number may play this game. (If the group numbers more than twenty, it should be divided.) Children join hands in a circle. One person is designated the leader, and the two persons directly opposite him in the circle are designated the archmakers.

Game

Meas. 1–2   Everyone walks forward four steps to center, raising their arms as they walk.

Meas. 3–4   They walk backward four steps, lowering arms.

Meas. 5–8   Repeat the first four measures.

Meas. 9–16   *Everyone keeps hands joined. The archmakers raise their joined hands to form an arch. The leader crosses the circle and walks under the arch, pulling the others (including the arch makers) behind him.* (The entire group will have formed a circle inside out.)

Meas. 1–4   As the song is sung again, all walk backward four steps, raising arms, then forward, lowering them.

Meas. 5–8   Repeat the above.

Meas. 9–16   To return the circle to its original position, the leader walks backward through the arch with everyone following, hands still joined.

Meas. 1–8   Repeat the steps which were done at the beginning.

Old Brass Wagon (Grades 1, 2, 3)

Formation

Assign a separate singing group.

Dancers join hands in a circle. Each boy should have a girl partner on his right.

Game

Stanza 1   All walk (or skip) to the left.

Stanza 2   All walk (or skip) to the right.

Stanza 3   *Partners face, join right arms at the elbow, and skip eight counts around in place. They change to left arms and skip eight counts the other way.*

Stanza 4   Partners make a double circle facing counterclockwise. (Girls will be on the outside.) Boys cross hands and join hands of their partners. All walk.

Stanza 5   Partners drop hands. Boys turn and walk clockwise; girls continue to walk counterclockwise. On the last two measures, all stop walking. The boys claim the girls beside them as new partners.

Stanza 6   Couples swing with new partners as in stanza 3.

Old Brass Wagon

Midwest Singing Game

First note : G   Piano : L-R-R-R   Chords : G, D7, C

2. Circle to the right, old brass wagon. . . .
3. Swing, oh, swing, old brass wagon. . . .
4. Promenade right, old brass wagon. . . .
5. Walk it up and down, old brass wagon. . . .
6. Break and swing, old brass wagon. . . .

Chimes of Dunkirk (Grades 1, 2, 3)

Formation

Assign a separate singing group.

Dancers make a double circle of partners, boys on the inside facing girls on the outside.

Dance

Meas.   1–2   All stamp feet three times and wait one count.
Meas.   3–4   All clap hands three times above their heads and wait one count.

Chimes Of Dunkirk

J. L. R.   French Folk Dance

We stamp up - on the ground,   Then
Hel - lo! How do you do?   And

make a clap - ping sound;   We take our part - ners
may I dance with you?   While chimes of Dun - kirk

Fine

by the__ hand and swing a - round.
ring a__ mes - sage loud and true.

Refrain

It's for - ward, back, and so,   We

bal - ance to and fro;   We swing our part - ners

D.C.

once a - gain, Then on we go.

Meas.   5–8   *Partners join both hands and skip around once in place.*
Refrain:
Meas.   9–10   *Partners take right hands and put free hands on hips. They step on right foot (two counts), then put weight on left foot (two counts). (Balance step)*
Meas. 11–12   Repeat balance step.
Meas. 13–14   Partners join both hands and skip around once in place.
Meas. 15–16   All drop hands and take one step left to face new partners.
Meas.   1–8   Repeat the steps of the first eight measures with the new partners.

(Grades 2, 3, 4)

Navajo Happy Song

Navajo Indian Song

Hi yo hi yo ip si ni yah, Hi yo

hi yo ip si ni___ yah, Hi___ yo hi yo ip si

Repeat twice

ni yah, Hi___ yo hi yo ip si ni yah,

Ip si ni YAH!

The following directions are not for a specific dance. Rather, they are some of the formations, steps, and motions performed in various American Indian dances. The children may choose from the suggestions and create a dance in Indian style.

Possible Formations

1. A single file which follows the winding path of a leader
2. Parallel lines of dancers
3. Dancers in a single circle (as if around a campfire)

Steps

1. Step, hop, hop, hop for one measure, first to the right, then to the left.
2. Toe-heel by stepping on the ball of one foot for the first beat and bringing the heel of the same foot down on the second. Repeat, using other foot, and so forth.
3. Step-hop on right foot while left arm swings high; step-hop on left foot, swinging right arm high.
4. Move forward with small leaps on one foot, then the other.
5. Step right (count one), bend both knees (count two), step left (count three), bend both knees (count four).

Additional Suggestions

1. Dance with arms folded across chest.
2. Raise arms to sky as if singing about sun, rain, etc.
3. Dance with bells fastened to ankles.
4. Move arms up and down as if punching the ground while dancing.
5. Alternate group dancing by having individuals create solo dances.

Christmas Dance (Grades 2, 3, 4)

Christmas Dance

J.L.R.   Swedish Folk Dance

First note : G   Piano : L-R-R   Chords : G, D⁷

Christ - mas time is here, the sea - son of good cheer,
Tra   la   la   la la, tra la   la la   la la

When hap - py peo - ple join the danc - ing,
Tra   la   la la   la la la la_____ la,

1·2 Part - ners in a row, back_ and forth they go,

At each oth - er they are glanc - ing.

3. Couples circle round;
   They make a joyous sound
   To wish each other "Merry Christmas!"
   'Round the circle so, back and forth they go,
   Wishing all a Merry Christmas.

4. Tra la la la la, tra la la la la la,
   Tra la la la la la la la la,
   'Round the circle so, back and forth they go,
   Wishing all a Merry Christmas.

   Formation

Assign a separate singing group.

There may be as many dance groups as desired. A group should consist of two lines of two couples each. Partners join hands. Line One faces Line Two. They are about ten feet apart.

   Dance

Stanza 1   Line Two stands still while Line One takes nine slow running steps forward and stamps twice in place. Line Two runs backwards with nine steps, ending with two stamps.

Stanza 2   Line One stands still while Line Two repeats the steps.

Stanza 3   The head couples of both lines join hands to make one circle while the foot couples join hands to make another. They take nine slow running steps clockwise and stamp twice in place. This is repeated counterclockwise.

Stanza 4   All the dancers in the group join hands to make one large circle. They run clockwise nine steps, stamp twice in place, and repeat this counterclockwise.

Ach, Ja! (Grades 2, 3, 4)

   Formation

Assign a separate singing group.

Partners make a double circle facing counterclockwise, boys on the inside, girls on the outside. They join adjacent hands.

   Dance

Meas. 1–2   All walk forward four slow steps.

Meas. 3–4   Partners drop hands, face each other and bow once, turn back to back and bow again.

Meas. 1–4   Repeat the above.

Meas. 5–6   *Partners face each other and join both hands. Continuing counterclockwise, they take a step in that direction, then slide the other foot to the first, swinging their arms ahead of them, then back.* They make a total of four step-slides, then turn.

Meas. 7–8   Repeat the above, moving in a clockwise direction.

Meas. 9   Partners drop hands, face each other and bow.

Meas. 10   Girls stand still while boys take one step counterclockwise to the next girls. All bow to new partners.

The dance is repeated with the new partners.

Ach, Ja!

J. L. R.   German Folk Dance

First note : low D   Piano : L-R   Chords : G, D7, C

When the fa-ther and the moth-er at the church do call,
Al - tho' they're lack-ing mon-ey no one cares at all,

Ach, ja! Ach, ja!

Refrain

Tra la la, tra la la, Tra la la la la la la,

Tra la la, tra la la, Tra la la la la la la,

Ach, ja! Ach, ja!

Hawaiian Boat Song

Formation

Assign a separate singing group. It is customary for girls to do the dancing. They should kneel, sitting low on their heels. Or, they may stand and sway hips while telling the story of the song with their arms and hands.

Dance

Meas. 1–2 Place right arm in front of waist, hand open, palm down. Left arm, hand, and fingers should point up like the mast of a boat. Body sways with music.

Hawaiian Boat Song

J. L. R.

Hawaiian Folk Song

First note : low B

Piano : L-R

Chords : G, D7

① G · Our boat is glid - ing, glid - ing, glid - ing,

Our boat is glid - ing o - ver the wa - ter.

⑤ G · Our boat is glid - ing, glid - ing, glid - ing,

Our boat is glad - ing o - ver the sea.

⑨ D7 · White clouds are roll - ing a - cross a blue sky,

While o - ver - head a rain - bow bright - ens.

⑬ D7 · The rain - bow reach - es a - cross the moun - tain,

And in our boat we glide o'er the sea.

Meas. 3–4	Moving from left to right, make wavy motions with both hands to indicate waves.
Meas. 5–8	Repeat all of the above.
Meas. 9	Arch both arms over head, and roll hands in the air one over the other to show the rolling of clouds.
Meas. 11–12	Slowly raise arms to shape the arch of a rainbow.
Meas. 13	Swing arms in an arc from left to right.
Meas. 14	Make a "mountain peak" in the air with both hands, fingers touching.
Meas. 15	Show a "boat" as in measures 1-2.
Meas. 16	Show the rippling of water as in measures 3-4.

Minuet from "Don Juan" (Grades 3, 4, 5)

Formation

Assign a separate singing group.

Any number of couples are arranged in a line or a circle. The girls are on the boys' right, inside hands joined. The boys put free hand on hips; the girls hold their skirts with outside hands.

Dance

Meas. 1	Beginning with inside foot, all walk forward three steps.
Meas. 2	Point outside foot forward and hold three counts.
Meas. 3–4	Repeat, starting with outside foot.
Meas. 5–6	Repeat, starting with inside foot.
Meas. 7–8	Partners face each other and drop hands. Boys bow from the waist and girls curtsy for six full counts.
Meas. 1–8	Couples turn and repeat the above eight measures, moving in the opposite direction.
Meas. 9	*Partners face each other, join right hands and hold them high. They step forward on right foot (count one), bring left foot to right and rise on toes (count two), drop back on heels (count three).*
Meas. 10	*Step on left foot (count one); point right foot forward (counts two and three).*
Meas. 11–12	Repeat measures 9–10 (balance step).
Meas. 13–14	*Keeping right hands joined and raised, partners walk halfway around each other, stepping right, left, right. They point left toe (three counts).*
Meas. 15–16	Partners face. Boys bow and girls curtsy for six counts.
Meas. 9–16	Repeat measures 9–16 above, and return to original formation.

Minuet from "Don Juan"

J. L. R.   W. A. Mozart

When Wash - ing - ton was pre - si - dent,

Peo - ple were care - ful and__ cor - rect;

Dressed in the cos - tumes of the day,

They danced the min - u - et.

La - dies in hoops and men in wigs,

Can you not see them danc - ing now?

Step - ping care ful - ly and point - ing toes,

Then end - ing with a bow.

Pop! Goes the Weasel (Grades 3, 4, 5)

Formation

Assign a separate singing group.

There may be as many sets of dancers as desired. A set consists of three couples, the three girls in a line facing the three boys about four feet apart. The couple nearest the audience is the head couple.

Pop! Goes the Weasel

American Folk Dance

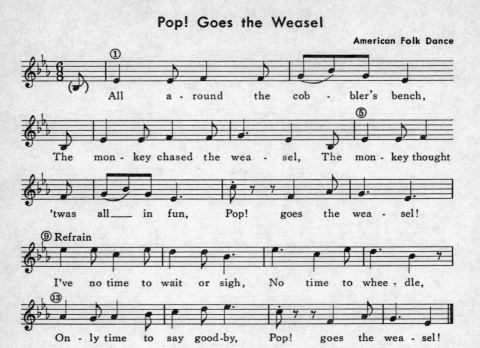

All a-round the cob-bler's bench,

The mon-key chased the wea-sel, The mon-key thought

'twas all__ in fun, Pop! goes the wea-sel!

Refrain

I've no time to wait or sigh, No time to whee-dle,

On-ly time to say good-by, Pop! goes the wea-sel!

2. A penny for a spool of thread,
   A penny for a needle,
   That's the way the money goes;
   Pop! goes the weasel!
        (Refrain)
3. From round about the countrymen's barn,
   The mice begin to mizzle;
   For when they poke their noses out,
   Pop! goes the weasel!
        (Refrain)

Dance

Stanza 1

    Meas. 1–2   *The head boy and girl turn toward the audience and continue turning until they face the foot of their respective lines. They*

	skip four skips down the outside of the set, stopping at the foot.
Meas 3–4	*They turn and skip behind their own lines back to place.*
Meas. 5–6	*The head couple turns to the foot inside the set and joins inside hands. They skip four skips to the foot.*
Meas. 7–8	*They turn, change hands, and skip back to place.*
Meas. 9–14	The head couple then joins hands with the girl second in line and they circle counterclockwise 12 counts.
Meas. 15–16	*The head couple raises joined hands to form an arch. On the word "Pop!" the girl is pushed under their raised arms and back to her place. (This should be planned ahead so that the person being "popped" ends up at his place and not just any-where!)*
Stanzas 2–3	As the song continues, the head couple circles with the boy second in line (see directions for circling in measures 9–16). They circle with the third girl and, finally, with the third boy, ending at the foot of the set. From this position, the head couple repeats the directions for measures 1–8 of stanza 1 above, ending at the foot and remaining there. The second couple will now be the head couple. The dance is repeated twice again to give each couple a turn at being head couple.

Cshebogar (Grades 3, 4, 5)

Formation

Assign a separate singing group.

Partners join hands in a circle, girls to the right of boys. Dancers should imagine that they are moths and that there is a flame in the center of the circle.

Dance

Meas. 1–8	All *step-slide* to the left eight times.
Meas. 1–8	Repeat, moving to the right.
Meas. 9–10	All walk to the center in four steps.
Meas. 11–12	Walk backward four steps, ending with a stamp.
Meas. 13–16	Partners hook right arms at the elbows and skip around eight steps in place.
Meas. 9–12	All drop hands and walk cautiously to the center in eight steps.
Meas. 13–16	Turn and run quickly back to place. At the end, every-one should raise his right fist and shout "Hey!"

Cshebogar

J. L. R.   Hungarian Folk Dance

First note : A   Piano : L-R   Chords : F, C7

Step - slide,___ step - slide,___ care - ful - ly;
Step - slide,___ step - slide,___ right we go;

Step - slide,___ step - slide,___ cau - tious be.
Step - slide,___ step - slide,___ end - ing so.

Walk in to the cen - ter and then
Once a - gain you walk - up to the

all walk back to place, With your part - ner
cen - ter of the ring, Has - ten back to

turn a - bout, as you dance face to face.
find your place be - fore the flame can sting! Hey !
(shout)

The Crested Hen (Grades 3, 4, 5)

Formation

Assign a separate singing group.

Sets of three dancers each join hands to form small circles. If possible, there is a boy in the middle and there are two girls at the sides. All sets face counterclockwise in a large circle.

The Crested Hen

J. L. R.

Danish Folk Dance

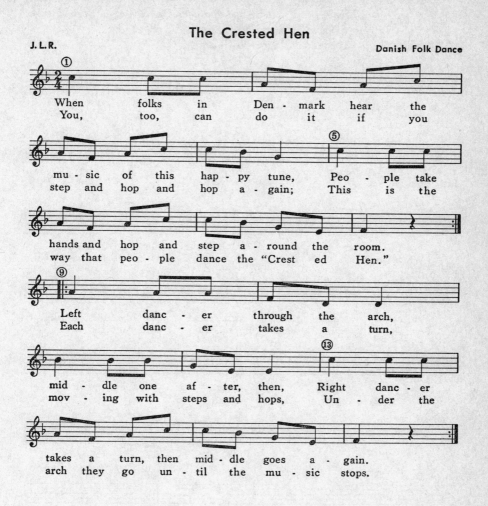

When folks in Den - mark hear the
You, too, can do it if you

mu - sic of this hap - py tune, Peo - ple take
step and hop and hop a - gain; This is the

hands and hop and step a - round the room.
way that peo - ple dance the "Crest - ed Hen."

Left danc - er through the arch,
Each danc - er takes a turn,

mid - dle one af - ter, then, Right danc - er
mov - ing with steps and hops, Un - der the

takes a turn, then mid - dle goes a - gain.
arch they go un - til the mu - sic stops.

Dance

Meas. 1–8   All *step-hop* forward eight times.

Meas. 1–8   Repeat, going in the opposite direction.

Meas. 9–12   *The two side dancers (girls) drop joined hands. The dancer to the right of middle and the middle one (the boy) make an arch with their joined hands. Still step-hopping, the left dancer goes under the arch, followed by the middle dancer.*

Meas. 13–16   *The dancer on the left and the middle one make an arch with their joined hands, and the dancer on the right goes through followed by the middle dancer.*

Meas. 9–16   Repeat measures 9–16 above.

Peasant Dance (Norway) (Grades 4, 5, 6)

Formation

Assign a separate singing group.

Dancers hold hands in groups of three, the middle person leading. Preferably the middle person is a boy with two girls at his sides. The leader holds the outside hands of the other two, and they join their inside hands behind his back. (The leader may hold two handkerchiefs instead of the hands of the others.) Groups move counterclockwise in a circle.

Dance

Meas. 1–8	Starting on the right foot, the groups move forward with a *stamp-run-run step*.
Meas. 9–10	*Bending low, the leader runs backward under the arms of the others and takes three running steps in place.*
Meas. 11–12	*The dancer on the leader's right turns in place under his right arm, using six running steps.*
Meas. 13–14	*The dancer on the leader's left crosses in front of him and also goes under his right arm with six steps.*
Meas. 15–16	*The leader turns to the right and with six running steps goes under his own right arm.*
Meas. 1–8	Repeat from the beginning with stamp-run-run step.

Hora (Grades 4, 5, 6)

Formation

A separate singing group is optional.

Dancers make two large circles of the same size, one inside the other. They face center and put their hands on their neighbors' shoulders. The two circles should move in opposite directions. The dance is often performed in bare feet.

Dance

Directions are for the inside circle which moves right. Outside circle moves in the opposite direction, reversing the directions.

Meas. 1	*All step to the right on right foot; place left foot in back of right and step; step right again; hop right while kicking left foot forward.*
Meas. 2	*Step left, right, left and hold.*

These two measures are continued throughout the dance, the tempo gradually increasing at the end.

Hora

J. L. R.

Palestinian Folk Song

Work - ers,   their la - bors   end - ed,   join in a
Slow - ly,   the mu - sic   coax - ing,   the cir - cle

1. cir - cle   to step an   an - cient dance.   **2.** hop and prance.
weav - ing,   the dan - cers

In an - cient Pal - es - tine,   peo - ple   danced arm on   arm,

Step - ping   and hop - ping   to   mu - sic   of old.

Gradually accelerate

Dance   to   the ho - ra mu - sic, dance   to   the ho - ra mu - sic,

Fast - er   and fast - er mov - ing, fast - er   and fast - er mov - ing,

In and out,   in   and   out,   In hap - pi - ness   the peo - ple shout!

Polka (Grades 4, 5, 6)

Formation

Assign a separate singing group.

Partners make a double circle facing clockwise, girls on the inside. They join adjacent hands and put free hands on hips.

Polka

J. L. R.

Czechoslovakian Folk Dance

First note : B   Piano : L–R   Chords : G, D7, C

Heel - toe, heel - toe, pol - ka we're danc - ing;

Heel - toe, heel - toe, al - ways ad - vanc - ing.

Part - ners at each oth - er are glanc - ing,

As they move to mu - sic en - chant - ing.

Refrain

Tra la la la, tra la la la,
Tra la la la, tra la la la,

Peo - ple love to dance and to sing.
Mu - sic helps us whirl 'round the ring.

Dance

Meas. 1–2   *All touch heel, toe, heel, toe, starting with outside foot.*
Meas. 3–4   *Starting with outside foot, take one polka step forward—step,*
             step, step, hop.

Meas. 5–8	Repeat the above, starting with inside foot.
Meas. 9–16	Repeat all of the above.
Refrain:	Partners face. Boys put both hands on girls' hips; girls put both hands on boys' shoulders. *They polka around the circle in couples.*

Turkey in the Straw (Virginia Reel) (Grades 5, 6)

Formation

Assign a separate singing group or use the record in RCA Victor "Rhythmic Activities," Volume V, of "Turkey in the Straw."

There may be as many sets of dancers as desired. A set consists of from four to eight couples, the girls in a line facing the boys about six feet apart. The head couple is nearest the music.

2. Went out to milk and I didn't know how,
   I milked the goat instead of the cow.
   A monkey sittin' on a pile of straw
   Was a-winkin' at—his—mother-in-law.

Dance

Meas. 1–4	The boys' line, with joined hands held high, skips forward four skips toward the girls' line and skips four skips backward to place.
Meas. 5–8	The girls' line repeats.
Meas. 9–12	*All skip forward, partners join right hands, skip once around each other and return backward to place.*
Meas. 13–16	Repeat, using left hands.
Meas. 1–4	Repeat, using both hands.
Meas. 5–8	*All fold arms, skip forward and docey-do, passing right shoulders, and skipping backward to place.*
Meas. 9–12	Repeat docey-do, passing left shoulders.
Meas. 13–16	The head couple joins both hands and takes four step-slides to the foot of the lines and back.

Reel

Use four measures for each motion.

The head couple joins right hands and turns around each other, extending left hands. The girl grasps the left hand of the second couple boy while the boy grasps the left hand of the second couple girl. They swing once around until the head couple meets in the center where they join right hands and swing around, extending left hands. They grasp the left hands of the third couple and swing once around with them, and continue thus until all other couples

Turkey in the Straw

American Folk Song

First note : A   Piano : L–R   Chords : F, C⁷, B♭

As___ I drove down a - long the road

With a tir - ed team and a heav - y load,

I___ cracked my whip and the lead - er sprung,

Says___ I good - bye___ to the wag - on tongue.

Refrain

Tur - key in the straw, Tur - key in the hay,

Tune up the fid - dles, Doo - dle de day,

Roll 'em up 'n' twist 'em up a high tuck - a - haw,

And___ hit 'em up a tune___ called___ Tur - key in the Straw.

have been swung. The head couple then joins hands and takes four step-slides back to place, drops hands, and returns to lines.

Cast-off

The girls' line faces the head girl while the boys' line faces the head boy. Going outside their lines, the head boy and head girl lead the lines to the position of the foot couple. They meet and form an arch with both hands joined. The boy and girl immediately behind them join inside hands and pass under the arch, followed by the other couples in order. The second couple skips to the position of head couple. All drop hands and fall back into the lines. The original head couple stays at the foot, and the dance is repeated with the original second couple as the new head couple. The dance may be repeated until all have had turns at being head couples.

Hat Dance (Grades 5, 6)

Assign a separate singing group.

A. JARABE (Ha-RAH-bee)

Formation

Dancers make a double circle of partners, girls on the inside. Boys hold their own hands behind their backs while girls hold their skirts.

Dance

All step alternately on: (1) *right heel,* (2) *left toe,* (3) *right toe,* (4) *left heel.* Continue for the remainder of the music.

B. SIDE-STEP

Formation

Dancers face clockwise in their double circle, girls still on the inside. As they dance, girls will move toward the center of the circle, boys away from the circle edge.

Dance

Meas. 1–2   *Step on toe of foot nearest partner (count one); moving away from him, stamp on other foot (count two). Repeat toe step, stamp for both measures.*

Meas. 3–4   *Repeat toe step and stamp; touch heel of first foot to floor, toe pointing toward partner, for two counts. Touch toe of first foot in front of the other (one count); rest weight on both feet (last count).*

Hat Dance

J.L.R.

A. Jarabe

Mexican Folk Dance

First note : high D   Piano : L-R   Chords : G, D7

With our friends we will dance the jar - a - be,

On this Mex - i - can fes - ti - val day,___

In se - ra - pes and wide - brimmed som - bre - ros,

All the peo - ple are laugh - ing and gay.

B. Side Step

First note : high C   Piano : L-R-R   Chords : F, C

Ev - 'ry - one in fan - cy cos - tumes,

Swing - ing sway - ing, with the danc - ing,

Part - ners smil - ing at each oth - er,

1. First re - treat - ing, then ad - vanc - ing.

2. First re - treat - ing, then ad - vanc - ing.

C. Hat Dance

First note : A   Piano : L-R   Chords : F, C⁷

Mu - sic quick - ens, cou - ples dance A - round the

wide som - bre - ros weav - ing, Get en - cour - age - ment from

watch - ers Whose ap - plause they are re - ceiv - ing.

D. Finale

First note : C   Piano : L-R   Chords : F, C

O - le! O - le! The mu - sic has been so

gay, O - le! O - le! We

danced all our cares a - way! (On repeat, shout Ole!)

72

Meas. 5–8   Return to position by starting with foot away from partner and performing steps in reverse.

Meas. 1–8   Repeat the above.

C. Hat Dance

Formation

Boys should toss a large hat or sombrero, if available, on the floor in front of their partners' feet. Girls turn their backs to hats, facing right. Boys follow their partners.

Dance

Boys and girls perform the same steps, except that boys do not touch the hats.

Dancers hop on right foot, crossing left foot behind so that the toe touches. (Girls touch left toe in hat brim.) They hop (girls in brim) on left foot while tapping right toe in front. They should move to the right while hopping. Steps are continued for the remainder of the music.

D. Finale

Formation

Boys pick up hats and place them on partners' heads. Girls hold onto them with both hands. Partners face, and boys put hands on hips.

Dance

Meas. 1   *All hop on left foot while bringing right heel to floor.*

Meas. 2   *Repeat, hopping on right foot, left heel to floor.*

Meas. 3–4   *Hop as above three times—left, right, left—with the music.*

Meas. 5–8   Repeat measures 1–4.

Meas. 1–8   Repeat the above. End by shouting "Ole!"

Black-Eyed Susie (Square Dance) (Grades 5, 6)

Formation

Assign a separate singing group.

Four couples form a square, all facing center, girls to the right of their partners. The first couple has their backs to the caller; first and third couples face. The second couple is to the right of the first; fourth couple is opposite second. The corner is on the boys' left.

2. Going home with lots of money,
   There's a little girl there to call me honey, etc.
3. My old dog's a bob-tailed daisy,
   Baying at the moon till he drives me crazy, etc.

Black-Eyed Susie

American Folk Song

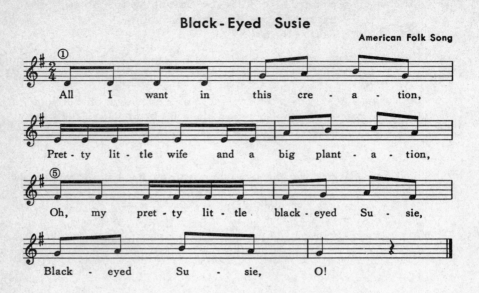

All I want in this cre - a - tion,

Pret - ty lit - tle wife and a big plant - a - tion,

Oh, my pret - ty lit - tle black - eyed Su - sie,

Black - eyed Su - sie, O!

4. I go hunting in the hollow,
   Possum's up a gum stump and I won't follow, etc.

Dance

All square dances start with the first call (below). Try various combinations of calls to become aquainted with them and to find suitable combinations for your group. The caller should say the first group of words and wait until the dancers have completed the steps before saying another call.

Calls

1. HONOR YOUR PARTNER, HONOR YOUR CORNER: Partners face and bow or curtsy; neighbors face and bow.
2. ALL JOIN HANDS AND CIRCLE LEFT; ALL JOIN HANDS AND CIRCLE RIGHT: Skip or walk eight counts in the direction named.
3. SWING YOUR CORNER; SWING YOUR PARTNER: *Corners link right arms at the elbow and skip, turning in place eight counts; partners link left arms and swing.*
4. DOCEY-DO YOUR CORNER; DOCEY-DO YOUR PARTNER: *Corners face and walk toward each other three steps, passing right shoulders; they step right, back to back, and walk backwards to place three steps.* Partners face and docey-do.

5. LADY ROUND THE LADY AND GENT ROUND THE GENT: *Second couple to right of the first separates and the first boy walks left around second boy while first girl walks right around the girl and back to place.*

6. GENT ROUND THE LADY AND LADY ROUND THE GENT: *First couple boy walks around the second couple girl while first couple girl passes around second boy.*

7. ALLEMANDE LEFT YOUR CORNER; ALLEMANDE RIGHT YOUR PARTNER: *Boys take left hands of corner girls and they walk once around each other; partners take right hands and walk around each other.*

8. ALLEMANDE LEFT, GRAND RIGHT AND LEFT: *Boys take left hands of corner girls and turn once around. Partners are now facing. They take right hands and walk past each other, passing right shoulders. All extend left hands to the next persons and pass left shoulders, continuing until all are back with partners.*

9. PROMENADE ALL: *Form a double circle facing counterclockwise, boys on the inside. Partners take right hands. Boys put left hand under to take girls' left hand in skating position. They walk or skip once around the circle and back to place.*

10. BALANCE: *Partners join hands, step left, swing right feet in front of themselves, step right and swing left feet across.*

11. ALL SWING: *Partners take dance position, right sides together. They pivot on right foot and push themselves around with their left.*

12. SWING IN THE CENTER, SIX HANDS AROUND: *The first couple swings in the center while the other couples join hands around them and circle to the left.*

Part Two

TEACHING SINGING

Singing is the musical activity which usually occupies most of the time of our school music periods. Part of the reason for this is that singing voices are with us, available at all times, and partly it is because singing is a natural and pleasurable form of human expression.

The infant discovers and experiments with his singing voice, as well as his speaking voice, while still in his crib. We hear him find all the sounds in the alphabet and more. We hear him holding onto singing sounds, making them short and sharp, making them loud, making them soft and cooing. Suddenly we hear a crescendo or a diminuendo. The sounds rise in pitch only to fall again.

Adults lead little children to convert the noises they make experimentally into words and speech, but only occasionally do adults ask them to sing. Often it is not until he gets to school that the child is expected to use his singing voice. Teachers are well aware that little children enjoy singing. Their voices may not range too far, either high or low, but it is the enjoyment of singing that most educators feel is of the greatest importance.

It is natural for children to like singing in school because they experimented with making singing sounds when they were babies. There are other reasons for its appeal. There is the joy of singing in a group. The group singing experience can help individuals feel secure and not alone. The participants hear their individual voices amplified to a larger, stronger group voice.

Beside feeling strength in the communal effort of group singing, each

77

singer feels the discipline of the music and the group. Voices must act in unison, each moving as fast or as slow, as high or as low as the others. The music disciplines in that there can be no hesitation, no doing a part over, no correcting mistakes. Singers in a group must forge ahead or hold back as the music demands.

Singing requires physical effort. There will be strain and tension one moment and relaxation the next. Because they must breathe deeply to increase oxygen intake, singing can leave participants feeling refreshed.

Singing as an Aid in All Teaching

The act of singing gives children enjoyment; through singing they sense what it means to be a member of a group and to be disciplined by the music and by the other singers. Singing can also help train them in other disciplines connected with voice production.

For instance, during the singing of songs, children can be expected to use good diction and to enunciate words clearly. If you cannot understand the words the children are singing, sing a phrase to them with your mouth almost closed. Then sing the phrase again, articulating the words clearly. The children will immediately realize that they must open their mouths if they are to be understood. If they persist in singing indistinctly, urge them to make more effort with a reminder like: "Open your mouths."

Children often encounter words unfamiliar to them in songs. Using new words in a song is an excellent way both to increase vocabularies and to learn to pronounce words correctly. Chances are, when you hear children pronouncing words incorrectly, they do not know their meanings. Have someone define these words and give the correct pronunciations before the song is sung again.

There are several ways in which the singing of songs can help children learn to read or improve their reading. The child who can read song words in the rhythm of the song will gain in his ability to read any words quickly and fluently. Pauses at the ends of song phrases will demonstrate phrasing; the holding of some words in songs will illustrate stress; singing some passages loud and others soft will teach the effectiveness of making contrasts. All of these are techniques of expression, and expression is a way of giving meaning to what is said or sung. Reading teachers can let songs help them teach syllabication, for in all songs, words with more than one syllable are divided.

Songs can help teach social studies. When children sing a Negro spiritual, they can feel the distress once felt by an enslaved people. When they sing a sad song from Russia, they can sense how the Russians must have felt when life was difficult and the weather unbearable. When they sing a lively, happy song from a mountainous country, they can feel the influence of an invigorating climate and rugged topography on the spirits of the people.

When teachers think of singing as an aid to teaching, they usually remark about the way it helps children release pent-up feelings. They know that singing can change the mood of a group. "I use singing to help my class relax," one will say. Or, "When my children are tired, I always have them sing a few songs." I have known teachers to use singing to help almost any situation from quieting a noisy group to stimulating an apathetic one.

Choosing Songs

The age and ability of the children in your class will help you decide what songs to choose for them to learn. Young or untalented children will be most comfortable with songs that do not range too high or too low and which have rhythms that are appealing without being complicated. For these classes, choose songs with words about happy or humorous situations. Challenge more capable children with songs with words that have more subtle meanings and that have a wide melodic range and intricate rhythms.

When choosing songs you should also consider the season of the year, special features of the month (rain in April), holidays of the month, countries or peoples being studied, etc. For ideas for planning, see "Using This Book."

Singing Lessons and the Musically Untrained Teacher

There are many teachers who are willing to have music lessons with their children, but who, when it comes to singing, feel inadequate. This feeling often stems from the fact that they never had any musical training or cannot play an instrument.

This book, and especially the chapters on reading music and accompanying songs, was written for those teachers who feel unsure of their ability. If you are one of these people, I urge you to try these lessons. It will give you great satisfaction to actually read the music of a song or to accompany your class on the piano or Autoharp. I hope the feelings of success and accomplishment which you should experience as you present these lessons will encourage you to continue to teach singing.

Starting Songs on Pitch

Everyone who teaches songs to children must have a way of starting them on or near the correct pitch. A song like "The Star-Spangled Banner" which ranges both high and low can soon cause difficulty if the right starting point has not been found.

There is a small percentage of people who have the ability to think the pitch of a note and reproduce it. Others can find the note they want on a piano or other instrument. But, for most people, the surest way of starting a song correctly is with a pitchpipe.

A pitchpipe is a small harmonica-type instrument which will fit in purse or pocket. The openings are labeled with the letter names of the notes. When one note has two names, as, for example, F♯ and G♭ or D♯ and E♭, both letter names will appear.

In some song books, the letter name of the first note will be written at the beginning of a song. With most books, you will have to figure it out. To do this, you must know the letter names of the lines and spaces of the staff. Starting at the bottom, space names are F, A, C, and E. The lines are E, G, B, D, and F, which can be remembered as the first letters of "Every Good Boy Does Fine." If the first note of a song is located below the staff, count backwards from the bottom line (E). The first space under the staff is D, the line below the staff is C, etc.

The group of sharps or flats at the beginning of the song is the key signature. To find out what notes are affected, you must figure out the locations of every sharp or flat. For example, if there are three sharps, the first will be located on the top line (F), the second in the third space (C), and the third in the space above the staff (G). This would mean that *all* F's, C's, and G's are to be sharped. If the first note of the song were on the C line below the staff, it would be C♯ and not C.

When purchasing a pitchpipe, you would probably find one that reproduces notes from C to C more useful than one that goes from E♭ to E♭ or from F to F.

Teaching the Concept of High and Low in Pitch

To young children, the words "high" and "low" refer only to the physical height of objects. They do not realize that these words can refer to pitch in music. You can teach the concept quickly by instructing the children to say or sing after you: "This is my low voice," in low tones, and: "This is my high voice," in high tones.

Voice Tone in Singing

When songs are taught by rote, children are expected to imitate the voice of the teacher. Children cannot copy the quality of tone or the volume of which most adults are capable, but an adult can usually produce voice tones in a light, unforced manner that can be imitated by children. When you sing to them, use a voice quality that can be approximated by the children.

Since the chief aim in having children sing in school is to get them to want to sing, you should not spend too much time trying for perfection in voice tone. Everyone should sing with confidence, spontaneity, and enthusiasm. Some children sing with gusto without being asked. Others sound like slaves dutifully moving through the motions of singing. Why are the latter so apathetic? Maybe it is because they were discouraged from expressing themselves at an earlier time in their lives. It is your job as their teacher to watch for signs of interest in singing, and, as much as possible, to praise the resultant efforts. Every time they sing fairly well, remark that they have done very well because, for them, this will be true. Try to avoid negative comments that might increase their feelings of failure and inadequacy.

Once the love of singing has been unquestionably established, it will be safe to criticize voice tones. When children become highly enthusiastic, there is every chance that many will try to sing too loudly. When this happens, tell the children that the voice sounds they are making belong out-of-doors because when people sing or speak indoors, the walls, floor, and ceiling echo the sounds from their surfaces and make them louder. For this reason, people use quieter voices when indoors.

Dealing with Out-of-Tune Singers

Out-of-tune singing is a complex problem which requires considerable time if dealt with in full. If your group is enthusiastic about singing, it is probably wise to leave the question alone. However, here are a few comments about the problem and suggestions for quick treatment of out-of-tune singing.

Most adults who do not sing in tune are aware that they are not doing what they should, but the child who sings inaccurately often does not know it, simply because he does not know what is expected of him. Explain to such a child that he has "both a low voice and a high voice" and that he should use his high voice. This explanation is not accurate, but he will know what you mean and will sit higher, increase his effort, and sometimes bring his voice up to pitch. Even if he raises his voice only a degree higher, it will be an improvement which deserves praise. While the class is singing, go to the place of a child who is out-of-tune and suggest, "Sing higher," or, "Use your high voice."

Sometimes a child is in a group that sings so loudly he cannot hear his own voice. Many children who sing perfectly when alone lose this ability when singing with the group. Such a problem is usually outgrown by fourth grade. If it persists into upper grades, certain measures may be taken.

People who sing off pitch often appear not to be trying hard enough, and this is sometimes true. But, more often, the out-of-tune singer is exerting too much tension rather than too little. He has locked his muscles in the way that a runner tenses himself at the starting line. If he neglects to release the muscles needed for running when the gun goes off, he will remain immobile. The singer with an abbreviated voice range is so busy holding himself in check, he forgets to release the muscles he needs for singing.

To produce a high tone in music requires tension. The trumpet player must tighten his lips; the violin player must press his finger hard on the string; and the singer must make his vocal cords vibrate at a high frequency.

If your class sings out-of-tune, exercises might help free the muscles they need to produce high singing tones. These can be done in the school-room at desk places and should be as vigorous as space will allow. Have everyone stand and jump like jumping jacks ten or twenty times, or run in place, or make wide arm swings in rhythm. The exercise should involve as much of the body as possible.

Teaching a Song by Rote

When children are to learn a song from you which is not in their books, motivate their desire to learn it by discussing and asking questions about the subject matter before you begin. Tell them that you will ask them questions when they have finished singing it or that they should listen for something specific in the words. Sing the whole song and ask at least one question about it. If the song is long or otherwise difficult, repeat the procedure. (Do not let the children sing with you.) After you have sung it once or twice, ask for definitions of difficult words.

If the song is easy, the children may be asked gradually to help you sing it. For instance, they might fill in the last words of some of the phrases. Sing up to the word you want them to supply and hesitate. They will be eager to help you fill it in. Or, tell them that when you sing the song the next time, you want them to help you sing a phrase. Choose one that is interesting or humorous or difficult or that is the last one in the song. Sing it to the children and have them sing it to you. When you sing the song again, signal them to join you on the newly-learned phrase.

Now teach the rest of the song one phrase at a time. Train the children to sing *after* you, never with you. Tell them to wait until you have had your turn, or to imitate you or echo what you have sung. If a phrase is too long for the children to remember all of it, have them learn the first half, then the other half, then the whole thing. Continue teaching phrase by phrase.

Drilling Songs to Learn Them

Learning is reinforced by repetition. Songs that are to be learned must be sung again and again, and this can become tedious. Part of the job of teaching is to keep students from becoming bored, and you can accomplish this by varying the drill technique. Here are suggestions for drilling phrases in different ways: (1) Have individual children sing alone. (2) Have the phrase sung by different rows of children. (3) Ask the boys to sing, then the girls, then everybody. (4) Divide the class in half; have one side sing to the other and vice versa. (5) Have everyone sing loudly, then softly. (6) Ask everyone to sing the words, then hum the tune, then sing the words again.

Correcting Mistakes in Tunes

Most music we hear for the first time reminds us of other music learned previously. Children will be inclined to make the tune or the rhythm of a new song resemble another, or, if the song is difficult, they will look for the line of least resistance and try to simplify it in some way. For this reason, children should not sing with you while you are introducing a new song.

If you detect a part of a song that is being sung incorrectly, it is not always necessary to change it, especially if the children will not sing it much in the future. But if the song will be heard by other people or be sung later in life, or, if getting it right would benefit the learners, then the mistake should be corrected.

First, locate the phrase being sung incorrectly, and decide which is the first word the children are singing wrong. Sing the phrase and when you come to that particular word, hold it on the correct pitch for three or four seconds. Invite the children to imitate you, holding the word on pitch until you signal them to stop. The voices which had been singing incorrectly will be heard attempting to sing up or down to the pitch called for. Repeat the procedure until everyone can find the right pitch without hesitation. If the incorrectly sung word is near the beginning of a phrase, start the re-learning with the previous phrase. Since more work is involved in un-learning and re-learning than in original learning, you may have to review the whole process on another day.

If the children are having difficulty with the rhythm of a passage, show them how to do it correctly and drill the phrase as needed. If they are not sustaining a word that should be held, have them count the proper number of beats while they are singing the word.

Introducing Children to Music Books

Most publishers of music texts start the publishing of music books for children in second grade. Soon after children are given their first books, they should be led to make observations about the music. Following is a list of possible questions to ask:

1. What do we call the small round symbols, usually black, and usually with a short line going up or down from them? (Notes)
2. How many horizontal lines are drawn for the notes? (Five) How many spaces are between the lines? (Four) Notes can be placed on lines or in spaces, and the group of lines is called a staff.
3. (Draw a staff on the chalkboard and place a note on the bottom line.) How do you think this note will sound? (Low) (Put a note in the top space.) How will this note sound? (High) (Add a note on the middle line.) As I point, sing: "Low, high, middle."

4. Sometimes notes start low on the staff and "climb" up or start high and "climb" down, going from a line to the space above or below and then to the next line. (On a staff, start at the bottom line and draw eight notes going up.) What do we call these notes altogether? (A scale)

Teaching a Rote Song to Children with Books

When children first use music books, you must find out if they are following the words of songs with their eyes. Have them lay their books flat on their desks. You may tell them that the index finger of their right hand is their "music pointing finger" and that they should use it to show you that they can follow song words. They should place their fingers under the first word and, while the song is sung, push them along. (Check to see that this happens.)

If the song has more than one stanza written under the lines of the music, you must show the children how to read the words, or they will read them line by line the way they read a story. Again, books should be flat on the desks. Ask the children to point to the first line of words with their "music pointing fingers" and speak, not sing, them. Then have them point to the first word under the second line of music and tell you what it is. When all have found the proper place, they should point to and read the words of the second line. Follow the same procedure for the remaining lines. Then have the children go back to the beginning of the song and read the words of the second stanza in the same manner.

The only reason to have children point to song words with their fingers is to show you that they know where to look for them with their eyes. While they are learning a song or singing one, have them hold their books on the sides so that the lower midpoint rests on the desk and the upper part is tilted toward the eyes. With books in this position, eyes will not feel strain, posture will be good, and voices will come out into the room.

To motivate learning a new song, ask questions. Ask the children to name the song, tell you about any pictures on the page, tell about the subject matter, give meanings of new or difficult words, etc. Ask older children to tell the name of the country from which the music comes, to give information about the life of the people and how their way of living might contribute to the kind of music they produced. If the composer is noteworthy, his name should be given and, if they are pertinent to the song, facts about his life should be mentioned.

Teach rote songs phrase by phrase, having the children imitate you as when songs are taught without books for the children. After they have sung a song a number of times, the children will have it memorized and will be proud to sing it without books.

Teaching Songs with Records

Most of the publishers of music books have recorded many or all of the songs in their books. These are a godsend for many teachers, for now, they can teach songs unfamiliar to them which, in the past, they had no way of learning to sing.

If you use records for teaching songs, you should first motivate the children to learn as suggested in the paragraphs on teaching rote songs. Before you play the record of the chosen song, remind the children that they should not sing while it plays but should follow the words in their books if they have them. After they have listened, ask the children questions about the words, the meanings of difficult words, how the music makes them feel, etc. Repeat the procedure once or twice. Then put the record away.

On another day or at a later time that day, play the record again. If the song is very easy, invite the children to hum the tune. At another hearing, ask them to sing one particular phrase. Proceed very slowly over a period of days, allowing them to add one phrase at a time. Above all, do not hurry. This is teaching by the "whole song" method and should not be rushed.

If you can teach songs without records but still want to use them, play them to the children after the songs have been learned so they can compare their singing with that of the recording artists. Children usually want to sing along with records.

Dramatizing Songs

There are many characters in songs—kings and commoners, postmen and policemen, cats and mice—whose actions can be imitated by children. Children can also show how a leaf would fall or a train would move or a clock pendulum would swing as they sing about them. They can also undertake longer dramatizations of song stories.

Dramatizing songs can be uniquely beneficial to children, partly because the acting must be done within the limits of the music. For instance, when a song like "Three Blind Mice" is dramatized, the action must be timed to fit the music. The mice running, the farmer's wife chasing them, etc., are actions that must all be done at the moment they are being sung about. A play about the story might be short or long; the length of a play to music is predetermined.

Song dramatizations can give the aggressive show-off an opportunity to get the attention he craves. They can be a means for the fearful or quiet child to allow attention to be focused on him through the character he is portraying. Song dramatizations can give children a chance to sing alone in front of an audience.

When children dramatize a song, try to lead them without directing them. Suppose they have just learned a song about elephants. Ask them to imagine how it feels to be an elephant, heavy and bent over, with a trunk that swings slowly. Invite a few children to dramatize the song while the others sing. Single out children who performed well and have everyone watch them for a while. Then try it again with the same children. Next time give others a turn.

One of your most important jobs during song dramatizations will be to praise the children when they deserve it. Remember that acting which may appear mediocre might be highly significant to the child who is doing it. As you watch your group, do not hesitate to remind them, when necessary, that the music is there to guide them and that they must be careful to move with it.

Chapter 3

YOU CAN TEACH MUSIC READING

The sounds of music are represented on paper by music notes—black or white dots with short vertical lines leading from them. These are arranged on a set of five horizontal lines and, along with a few other symbols, constitute the code of music.

Two meanings are to be derived from the notes themselves. First, they indicate how fast or slow they are to be played or sung in relation to each other. Second, they signify where the sound is to be pitched, exactly how high or how low.

There is little in the appearance of a note to tell the unenlightened person how long to hold it. However, anyone might guess that notes which have been placed high on the staff of lines will sound high, while notes in a low position will have low sounds.

An instrument like the piano has its notes in a fixed position. However, when the instrument is the human voice, the singer must figure out where to pitch notes and how to relate them to one another. Fortunately, most people, children included, are able to sing the music scale. From this seemingly scant knowledge, it is possible to figure out almost any note interval.

For example, sing: "Do re mi do" twice. Add "mi fa so" and repeat. Do you recognize the song? You were singing the first part of "Are You Sleeping?" or "Frère Jacques." All songs are made up of note combinations like these. Anyone who would read music must first decode the written notes and then convert them into musical sound.

When to Start Song Reading in School

Because songs have words as well as music, a large part of song reading is word reading. This is one reason to put off the teaching of music reading until at least second grade. Another reason is that almost no books are published for first grade students. The lessons in this book have been written with children of second grade or higher in mind.

Teaching Music Reading with This Book

You will notice that the terms "quarter note," "eighth note," etc., are not used. Instead, words like "walk," "run," and "slow walk" are applied to describe the approximate rate of speed at which words with these notes over them should proceed. As soon as children have understood the rate of speed in terms of walking, etc., the proper terms may be presented.

The Latin, or so-fa syllable names, for notes are given rather than letters or numbers. Letter names are used by instrumentalists, and, since numbers are used to count beats in notes and to indicate time signatures, an additional use of numbers could be confusing. Perhaps the greatest advantage in learning to think with the Latin names is that the same seven names can be applied in any key. For instance, once you have learned to sing "do mi so," you will be able to sing it starting on any note. On the other hand, if you used letter names, you would have to change the letters every time you changed keys. In the key of F, you would sing "F A C," in the key of B♭, "B♭ D F," and so forth. Letter names give a singer little clue as to how to make the notes sound.

The lessons which follow suggest words which may be spoken in teaching. Motivation of lessons, review of material previously learned, etc., are not always given, and you should use your discretion about adding these to your presentations.

How to Picture the Music of the Songs

To present some of the lessons in song reading which follow, you will need chalk board space, or, if you plan to present the lessons frequently, you could make charts of the songs on large, sturdy paper.

To make staff lines on a chalk board, use a staff liner in which can be inserted five pieces of chalk for drawing the five lines simultaneously. If you do not have a staff liner, you can save time by drawing two lines at a time. Hold two pieces of chalk in your writing hand, one in the position you hold a pencil and the other about an inch below, securing both with your thumb. Draw both chalks across the board to make two equidistant lines.

To draw a G clef, make a straight line on the left side of the staff from just above the top line to just below the bottom one. Start back at the top and loop right, as if making a letter "P." Continue down, making a capital "G" which should end in a curl around the second, or G, line.

To make a picture of a quarter note with chalk, use a piece about an inch long and turn it sideways. Make a single diagonal stroke, moving the chalk downward from right to left. This is the note head. Attach a vertical stem, a line which is to the right of the note head if going up or to the left if going down. If you are picturing more than one such note at a time, make all the note heads first and attach the stems later.

When you write a song, use this sequence:

1. Draw the staff lines.
2. Draw the G clef, the key signature (sharps or flats), and the time signature.
3. Print the song words under the staff lines, hyphenating words of more than one syllable.
4. Draw the notes over the words. Notes above the middle staff line should have stems going down. Below the middle line, stems should go up.

MUSIC READING LESSONS

A. FEELING AND HEARING DIFFERENCES IN RHYTHM

Preparation for Lessons

It is optional whether or not the following poem is reproduced for the children to see.

First Lesson

———————————

What special way do people walk when they are in a parade? (They march) When people are all the same size, they can march together quite easily. But suppose an elephant and a mouse were in the same parade; they could never keep step with each other. Here is a poem which tells us what the animals did to keep together.

———————————

(Read "The Animal Parade," keeping your voice steady as you read the words with the notes over them.)

———————————

Which animals were able to keep time with the drum? (The horses) How did the largest animals keep themselves from moving too fast? (They walked twice as slowly as the horses.) What did the mice and chipmunks have to do to keep up? (They had to run.)

When I read the poem next time, I would like you to help me make

The Animal Parade

Down the street the animals come,
Marching proudly with the drum.

Trum   tum   tum   tum,   Trum   tum   tum   tum.

The elephant and grizzly bear
Walk slowly with a stately air

Slow   walk   slow   walk   Slow   walk   slow   walk

But mice and chipmunks have to run
To keep in time with everyone.

Run run   run run,   run run   run run,

Run run   run run,   run run   run

The horses as they walk on by
Hold their knees and heads up high

Walk   walk   walk   walk   Walk   walk   walk   walk

the sounds of the drum and of the animals' feet. We will use the palms of
our hands on our desks (or knees). To help us keep track of how many times
we say each word, every so often we will give a push to our voices. Try the
drum sounds after me: *Trum* tum tum tum, *Trum* tum tum tum. . . .

Now try: *Slow* walk, slow walk, *Slow* walk, slow walk. . . .

We must be careful when we say the "run" words. Listen first and try
after me: *Run* run run run, run run run run, *Run* run run run, run run
run. . . .

The horses go: *Walk* walk walk walk, *Walk* walk walk walk. . . .

Now I will read the poem. Wait until I come to the places where you
will help me with the sounds and then join in. . . .

Second Lesson

See if you remember how to make the sounds of the drum and of the animals in "The Animal Parade." As I read the poem, you may help me with the sound effects. . . .

I will say the poem again. This time you may say the words with me. (Help the children memorize the poem.)

Stand at your places. When we say the poem this time, let your feet keep time with the rhythm words instead of your hands. Your feet should not be moving when we say the poem words. . . .

Make a line around the room. . . . Imagine you are in the animal parade. Your feet will move even as you say the poem words. For instance, when you say: "The elephant and grizzly bear/Walk slowly with a stately air," what will your feet be doing? (Slow walk)

Listen to my voice. When I say "Forward march," you will start the poem. Mark time first—Trum tum tum tum, Forward march. . . .

B. Observing Rhythm in Notation

Preparation for the Lesson

The children should have music books at hand.

The Lesson

Sometimes music moves along slowly; sometimes it goes quickly. Sometimes it "walks" like the horses in "The Animal Parade."

We will sing the song "Are You Sleeping?"[1] As you are singing, listen for the words which your voices hold.

Did you hear the words which you held longer than the others? ("John" and "dong") When music writers want to show singers which words to hold or sing slowly, they put notes over the words like this: ♩ or ♪. Look in your music books until you find a song that has at least one "slow walk" note. (Children look in their music books for examples of half notes.)

I will choose one person to tell us the page on which he has found a "slow walk" note, and we will all turn to that page. . . . Tell us which word or words on this page must be sung slowly.

Sing "Are You Sleeping?" again. This time listen for the words which must be sung most quickly. . . .

Did you hear the words which went quickly, like the mice or chipmunks running? ("Morning bells are. . .") When words are to be sung fast, the notes over them look like this: ♫ ♫ or like this: ♪ ♪ Look in your books for a song with "run" notes. . . .

One person may tell us the page on which he found "run" notes. . . .

---

[1] If "Are You Sleeping?" is unknown to the group, substitute a song with the three rhythms being studied which will be known to all.

Let's turn to that page and be ready to tell which words must be sung fast. . . .

There are other notes in "Are You Sleeping?" They do not make us sing words very slowly or very fast, but rather like people walking. They look like this: ♩ or ♪ . Quickly find a song with "walk" notes in your books. . . . Put your pointer finger under one of the walk notes, and hold your book with your finger still pointing, under your chin. Keep it there until I have time to see that everyone is able to find a "walk" note correctly. . . .

C. Walk and Slow Walk Notes and Their Rests

First Lesson

I am going to write you a message on the chalk board, but, instead of using words, I shall write notes.

(Draw four quarter notes: ♩ ♩ ♩ ♩ .)

Do you remember what we called notes like these? (Walk notes) These are called "walk notes" because any words under them must be sung as fast as people walk. To read the note message, clap once and say "walk" for every note. Do this while I point to the notes. . . .

Here is more of the note message.

(Draw two half notes under the quarter notes: ♩ ♩ .)

What did we call these notes? (Slow walk notes) Notes like these tell us to sing the words over them as fast as someone walking slowly and are called "slow walk notes." When you clap and say this part of the message, clap only on the word "slow" and hold your hands together on "walk." Try it while I point to the notes. . . .

Clap and say the notes of the whole message from the beginning. . . .

Now clap the message four times without saying the rhythm names of the notes. . . .

Here is another note message.

♩ ♩ ♩ | ♩ ♩ ♩ | ♩ ♩ | ♩ ♩ ♩ ‖

Read this message two times. The first time, clap and say the notes while I point to them. The second time, clap them without speaking. . . .

Here is another message. Read it twice, the way you did the previous one. . . .

♩ ♩ ♩ | ♩ ♩ ♩ | ♩ ♩ | ♩ ♩ ‖

Here is one more message to read in the same way. . . .

♩ ♩ ♩ ♩ | ♩   ♩ ♩ | ♩ ♩ ♩ ♩ | ♩   ♩ ‖

Second Lesson

Here is the note pattern of a song which some of you will know:

♩ ♩ ♩ ♩ | ♩ ♩ ♩ | ♩ ♩ ♩ | ♩ ♩ ♩ ‖

♩ ♩ ♩ ♩ | ♩ ♩ ♩ | ♩   ♩ | ♩ ♩   ‖

Clap and say the notes as I point to them. Can you think of a song that has this rhythm pattern? (Children may try to guess if they wish.) Clap the pattern without saying the notes to see if you can guess what it is. . . .

You have just clapped the note pattern of "London Bridge." Sing the words and clap the pattern while I point to it. (The words are in Chapter 4. The first note is C.) . . .

Make a line (or circle) around the room. . . . As you sing, walk the rhythm pattern. Remember to stop on the slow walk notes. . . .

———————————

(Children return to seat places after walking.)

———————————

Look at the note pattern on the board. There is a music sign at the end. Can you guess what this sign tells us to do? (It tells us to stop or be quiet.) These signs are called rests. They tell people who are reading music to stop, maybe for a breath or for a short rest. When the rest is for as long as a walk note, it looks like this: ♩ . When it is for as long as a slow walk note, it looks like a small black hat: ▬ .

Here is a note pattern with rests in it.

♩ ♩ ♩ ♫ | ♩ ♩ ♩ ♫ | ♩ ♫ ♩ ♫ | ♩ ♩ ♩ ♫ ‖

You know how to clap and say notes. When you come to a rest, say the word "rest" while holding your hands apart, palms upward. Say and clap the notes and rests while I point to them. . . .

Clap the pattern without speaking it. . . .

Here is another pattern with rests:

♩ ▬ | ♩ ▬ | ♩ ♩ ♩ ♩ | ♩ ▬ ‖

When you come to these rests, hold your hands open while you say "slow rest." Clap and say the pattern while I point to it. Clap the pattern without speaking. . . .

The next note pattern contains all the different notes and rests we know:

♩   ♩ ⅂ |♩   ♩ ⅂ |♩   ♩ |♩   ▬   ‖

Clap and say the pattern while I point to it.... Clap the pattern without saying it....

D. Run Notes

The Lesson

When we sang "Are You Sleeping?" we noticed that some words went as fast as people walked; some went at a slow walk. How did the others go? (As fast as people run)

"Run" notes look like this: ♫ ♫ . (Draw on the chalk board.) How many notes do you see on the board? (Four) There are four notes because there are four heads and four stems.

Here is a note pattern with notes and rests.

♫♫♩ ⅂ |♫♫♩ ⅂ ‖

Clap and say the pattern.... Clap it without speaking....
Here is another pattern of notes. Try it in the same way....

♩ ♫♩ ♫|♩ ♩ ♩ ⅂ |♩ ♫♩ ♫|♩   ▬   ‖

Clap and say the last pattern.... Clap the pattern....

⅂ ♩ ♫♫|⅂ ♩ ♫♫|⅂ ♩ ♫♫|♩   ▬   ‖

E. Variations in Note Writing

Preparation for the Lesson

The children should have music books at hand.

The Lesson

Open your music books to the first song (or a song of your choice). The notes I have been picturing on the board for our music lessons have had stems going upward to the right of the note heads like this: ♩ or ♩ or ♫ . Look at this song to find notes with stems that go down, and be ready to tell what words are under them. (Children find examples.) When note stems go down, which side are they on? (Left) I will choose a person to make a picture on the board of a walk note with its stem going down, another to make a slow walk note, and someone else two run notes....

Can anyone guess from looking at the notes in the song why some notes are made with stems going up and some with stems going down? (If the children cannot answer, give them a clue.) Suppose a music writer was making notes on the bottom line of the staff. Would it be better if he made the stems go up or if he made them go down? (He should make them go up; otherwise they might run into the words below.) When notes are above the middle staff line, their stems go down, and when they are below the line, they go up.

The run notes we have been looking at have been joined together. Sometimes a music writer wants to picture separate run notes. Then he puts a short line called a flag on the end of each stem, like this: ♪ or ♩ . The rest for a run note looks like this: ƴ .

Look through your music books for a song that has the kinds of notes we know about—walk notes, run notes, and slow walk notes. The song may have the rests which go with these notes, but it should not have any other kinds of notes, including notes which have dots after them. . . .

Turn to the page chosen. . . . Lay your book open, flat on your desk. Place your pointing finger under the first note of the song. How fast does this note go? (Someone answers: "As fast as. . . .") We are going to say the time values of every note, pushing our fingers along as we say them. . . .

(Repeat the procedure with a different song.)

F. READING WORDS IN NOTE RHYTHMS

Preparation for First Lesson

Write the following poem on the chalkboard, leaving space above the words for notes to be written.

> Branch-es of trees
> That sway in the breeze
> Stay still in the night
> When breez-es are light.

First Lesson

Read the words of the poem together. . . .

If these words were the words of a song, there would be notes over them to tell singers how fast to go. For instance, here is one way the notes might tell people to say or sing the words.

Write notes over the words as follows:

First, clap and say the notes. . . .

Now we will read the words in the rhythm of the notes. As you read, part of your eye will see the word and part will see the note above it. (Let the children try this without help.) . . .

I am going to erase these notes and write in a different set.

Clap the notes first. . . . Now say the words in the new rhythm. . . .
Here is another way to say the words.

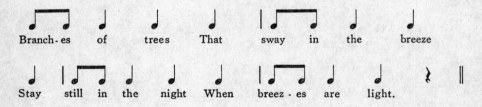

Preparation for Second Lesson

Write the following poem on the chalkboard, leaving space to write in notes above the words.

> Pud-dles are made
> For girls and boys
> To splash with their boots on,
> Splash with their boots on.

Second Lesson

Read the words of the poem together. . . .
Read the words the way these notes tell you. (Write notes.) . . .

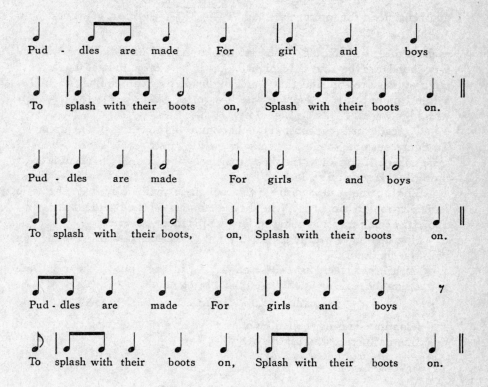

Pud - dles are made For girl and boys
To splash with their boots on, Splash with their boots on.

Pud - dles are made For girls and boys
To splash with their boots, on, Splash with their boots on.

Pud - dles are made For girls and boys
To splash with their boots on, Splash with their boots on.

G. THE MUSIC SCALE

First Lesson

Our lessons in music reading have thus far been teaching us how fast notes tell us to go. Music notes tell us something else. Do you know what it is? (They tell us how to sing the tune or how high or low to place our voices.)

To show us how high or how low to sing, notes are put on a set of lines. How many lines are used for music writing? (Five)

(Draw a staff of five lines on the chalk board.)

How many spaces are between the five lines? (Four) Sometimes notes are written "on" the lines, with the lines going through them. Sometimes they are written in the spaces between the lines.

Here is a note on the bottom line. (Draw   ) Here is another note in the top space. (Add   ) Can you guess how each of these will sound? (The first will sound low and the second high.) Low sounds are the kind that might be made by a large animal like a bear. High sounds are the kind that would be made by small animals like mice. While I point to the notes, sing with low voices: "This is a low note," then with high voices: "This is a high note." . . .

To read words, we must know the sounds of the letters of the alphabet. To figure out note sounds, we must know the music scale. There are seven scale names. If you know the music scale, sing it with me: Do re mi fa so la ti do; do ti la so fa mi re do.

Sing up the scale again, slowly enough so that I can write the scale names as you are singing. (Write the scale names on the board, starting just above the chalk tray and going vertically up, ladder fashion.)

Sing up and down the scale as I point to the scale names. (Do not sing with the children.)

To help you memorize these names, I will erase one of them and ask you to sing the scale again, filling in the missing name. . . .

(Continue erasing the names one or two at a time, having the children sing after each erasure, until the board is clean.)

Second Lesson

Sing the scale up and down from memory. . . .

Today we are going to see how the music scale looks when it is written on music lines. How many lines must I draw? (Five) (Draw a staff four or five feet across.) These lines together are called a staff. At the front of the staff is a G clef, a sign which tells us which is the G line of the staff. (Add a G clef to the staff.) These signs are called "flats." (Add three flats to the right of the G clef: .)

When notes are written on a staff, some of them are on lines. Where are the others? (In the spaces between the lines.) When you sang the scale, what was the lowest-sounding note? (Low "do") If I put low "do" on the first line, can you guess where "re" would be written? (In the space above, a little to the right) Where should the next note be written? (On the second line) Here is how the scale looks when it is written on a staff:

As I point to the notes, sing them from the music which has just been written. (Do not sing with the children.)

I will point to certain notes. Sing only what I point to. (Point to: "do re mi fa so" and stop; then "so la ti do"; "do ti la so"; "so fa mi"; "mi re do"; "do re mi re do," etc.)

H. A Song From Scale Segments

Preparation for the Lesson

Write the song, "Up and Down," either on large, heavy paper or on the chalk board.

Up and Down

Do — — — —

Up the scale we go,

— — — —

Then we drop down low.

The Lesson

At our last lesson, we saw how the music scale looks on a music staff. Look at the first line of this song. The first note is "do." What are the other notes? ("Do re mi fa so") Sing the first line of music. (Do not sing with the children.)

Why will the second line be easy to sing? (The notes are the same as those in the first line.) Sing the first line with notes; sing the second line with words and stop at the end. . . .

What is the name of the first note in the third line? ("So") Think the notes of the third line to yourselves. . . .

Why will the fourth line be easy? (It is the same as the third.) Sing the third line with notes and the fourth line with words. . . .

Sing the whole song as it is written. . . .

I. Songs with Repeated Notes

Preparation for the First Lesson

Write "Motion Song" on the chalk board or on paper.

Motion Song

Do — — — — — —

Clap your hands and slap your knee

— — — — — — —

Nod your head and tap your toe.

First Lesson

Look at the words of "Motion Song." What are you supposed to do with your hands? (Clap them and "slap your knee") What will your head do? (Nod) Your toe? (Tap)

The first note is "do." Say the note names in the first line while I point to every note. . . .

How many times must we sing "mi"? (Five times) Sing "mi" five times. . . . Now sing the first line of notes. . . .

Look at the third line. What is the name of the first note? ("Mi")
Say the note names in the third line while I point to them. . . .

How many times must we sing "do"? (Five times) Sing "do" five
times. . . . Sing the third line of notes. . . .

Which lines of notes are alike? (The first and second; the third and
fourth) If you can sing the first line with notes, you can sing the second with
words. You will sing the third line with notes, the fourth with words. Try
it. (Do not sing with the children.)

Sing the whole song, and do the motions. . . .

Preparation for the Second Lesson

Write "Tree Climbing" on the chalk board or on paper.

Tree Climbing

When you climb a tree that's high,

You must look up to the sky;

To get back you must look down

Till your feet are on the ground.

Second Lesson

Look at all of the notes in this song. How fast do most of them tell us
to go? (As fast as people walk) What words will be sung at another speed?
("high," "sky," "down," and "ground") How fast will they go? (At a slow
walk) Read the words of the song in the rhythm the notes tell you to go. . . .

What is the name of the first note of the song? ("Do") What is the second
note? ("Do") What are the names of all the notes in the first line? ("Do do
re re mi mi mi") When notes are repeated, they must sound alike. Sing "mi"
three times, keeping your voices at the same pitch. . . .

How is the next line of notes similar to the first? (The children should discuss the pattern of notes rising.) Are the last two lines similar to the first two? (Yes. They have the same pattern, but they go down rather than up the scale.)

Sing the song with notes. . . .

Sing the song with words. . . .

J. Songs with Note Skips

Preparation for the First Lesson

Write "Notes and Letters" on the chalk board or on paper. Plan to leave it for the next lesson.

Notes and Letters

First Lesson

In the song, "Notes and Letters," there are blank spaces at the beginning of each line. What note names belong in the spaces in the first line? ("re mi") In the second line? ("Mi fa so") Third? ("So fa mi") Fourth? ("Mi re do") To sing this song, sing the scale names at the beginning of each line, then the letters or words at the end of the line. Try it. . . .

Now we will sing the song in two groups. (Choose the groups.) Group

One will sing the notes, and Group Two will answer with the letters or words. . . .

Try it again. Group Two will start and Group One answer. . . .

───────────

Preparation for Second Lesson

The song, "Notes and Letters," will be used again. If it has been written on paper, make four paper inserts with the new notes to cover the notes of the first version of the song. If the song is on the chalk board, be prepared to erase the notes to be changed and to substitute the new ones.

Notes and Letters, 2

Second Lesson

───────────

Sing "Notes and Letters." (First version) . . .

I am going to make a little change in the notes of the first line. (Change the notes at the end of the line as shown.) Sing the notes (but not the letters) of the first line, making your voice skip the note that has been taken away. . . .

Watch while I change the notes of the other three lines so that you can learn to make those skips too. Try all the notes of the song this way. . . .

Sing just the last two notes of every line. (Children sing: "do mi, mi so, so mi, mi do." Review as needed.)

───────────

Preparation for Third Lesson

Write "Note Skipping" on the chalk board or on paper.

Note Skipping

Skip   one   note,   then   skip   one   more;

End   up   where   you   where   be - fore.

Third Lesson

At our last lesson we sang notes that did not go from note to note up the scale or down the scale. The notes we sang skipped other notes. Let's see if you remember them. Sing "do mi." . . . Sing "mi so." . . . "So mi." . . . "Mi do." . . .

Sing the notes of "Note Skipping." . . .

Sing the words of the song. . . .

Preparation for Fourth Lesson

Write the song, "Seesaw," on the chalk board or on paper.

Seesaw

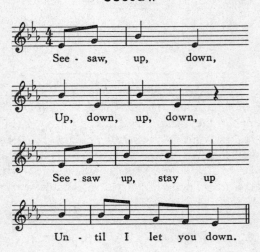

See - saw,   up,   down,

Up,   down,   up,   down,

See - saw   up,   stay   up

Un - til   I   let   you   down.

Fourth Lesson

Read the words of the song, "Seesaw," in the rhythm of the notes. . . .

Did you ever play on a seesaw and make the person who was playing with you stay up in the air? How did you do it? (The children discuss the questions.)

There is a place in the music of this song where we have to keep our voices up for a while like someone staying up on a seesaw. Can you find the notes where this happens? (At the end of the third line) Sing the notes of the third line. . . .

What are the first three notes of the song? (Do mi so) Sing them. . . . What is the next note? (Do) Sing the first line of notes. . . .

Why will the second line be easy to sing? (The notes are the same as the last two notes of the first line.) Sing the notes of the first and second lines. . . .

Sing the third and fourth lines with notes. . . .
Sing the notes of the whole song. . . . Sing the words. . . .

K. FIGURING OUT NOTE SKIPS

Preparation for First Lesson

Write the song, "Mathematics," on the chalk board or on paper.

Mathematics

Two and two and two are six,
Plus one more is sev - en.
Add six more and sub - tract two,
That will leave e - lev - en.

First Lesson

The tunes of the songs you have been reading have either gone up or down part of the scale, or they have made certain skips in the notes. In the first line of this song is a note skip which you have not seen before. Can you find it and name the notes? ("Fa re" at the end of the line is the new skip.)

Using what you already know about notes and the sounds of notes, how might you figure out the sounds of "fa re"? (By singing "fa mi re" and remembering the sounds of "fa" and "re") Let's try it. Sing "fa mi re." . . . Sing "fa re." . . .

As I point to the notes of the first line, think what their names will be and how they will sound. . . . This time when I point to the notes, sing them out loud. . . .

Study the second line to yourselves. . . . Sing the second line. . . .

Why will the third line be easy? (The notes are the same as those in the first line.) Sing the notes of the third line. . . .

Think the notes of the fourth line while I point to them. . . . Sing the notes of the fourth line. . . .

Look at the whole song. What words must be held longer than the others? ("Six," "seven," "two," and the last part of "eleven") Sing the whole song with notes. . . .

Sing the whole song with words. . . .

—————————————

Preparation for Second Lesson

Write "Bragging" on the chalk board or on paper.

Bragging

2. When I was seven,
   I flew up to heaven;
   When I was eight,
   I went sailing in a crate.

Second Lesson

———————————

Did you ever brag about yourself? Read the words of this song together to find out how the person in it was bragging about himself. . . .

Clap and say the rhythm of the notes of the whole song. . . .

Say the words of "Bragging" in the rhythm of the notes. . . .

Does the first line of notes have any skips you have never seen before? (No) Do you see any in the second line? (Yes. "La do la") How could you find how these notes will sound? (By singing "la ti do ti la" and remembering the sounds of "la do la") Try it. Sing "la ti do ti la." . . . Sing "la do la." . . . Sing the notes of the second line. . . .

Look at the last two lines. Can you find skips in the notes that you might not know? (We might not know "re fa" in the fourth line.) In the song, "Mathematics," you sang "fa re," but you have never sung "re fa." (If the children remember "fa re," they can learn "re fa," but it will probably be easier to use the system described above for finding unknown intervals.) Sing "re mi fa." . . . Sing "re fa." . . . Sing the notes of the fourth line. . . .

Sing the whole song with notes. . . .

Sing the song with words. . . .

———————————

L. Reading the Music of Songs in Other Keys

Preparation for First Lesson

Write "The Dragon and Me" on the chalk board or on paper.

The Dragon and Me

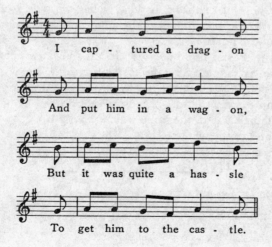

2. He squirmed and he wiggled,
   He giggled and he jiggled,
   But he gave up the battle
   When I made my tail rattle.

First Lesson

_____

The music of the songs we have been reading has had three flats in the key signature. (Show this on the chalk board: 𝄞♭♭♭ .) When there are

three flats, "do" is always on the first line, "re" is in the space above it, and so forth. But sometimes we want to sing a song higher or lower. Then we have to take all the notes and move them to a new position. "Do" will no longer be on the first line with "re" in the space above and "mi" on the line above that. There will be a different key signature, too.

Here is a song with "do" on the second line. The key signature is one sharp. (Show this on the chalk board: 𝄞♯ .)

_____

(*Note:* If any children want to know why key signatures change when the scale moves, have someone play the scale of C on the piano. Then ask him to begin the scale on another note, any note, and try to play it again. He will soon discover that he must use black notes to make it sound right. These black notes are the sharps and flats of key signatures.)

_____

If the first note of this song is "do," what will the second note be? (Re) As I point to the first line, say the note names in rhythm. . . . As I point again, sing the notes. . . .

Why will the second line be easy? (It has the same notes as the first, except there is an extra one.) Sing the first and second lines with notes. . . .

Study the notes of the third line to yourselves, thinking the name of each note and how it will sound. . . . Sing the third line. . . .

Study the fourth line in the same way. . . . Sing it. . . .

Sing the notes of the whole song. . . .

Sing the song with words. . . .

_____

Preparation for Second Lesson

Write "Rain Sounds" on the chalk board or on paper.

Rain Sounds

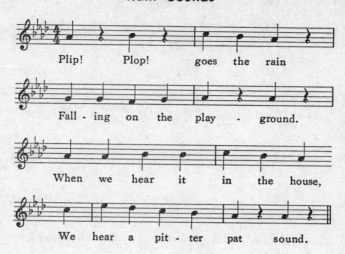

Plip!   Plop!   goes the rain

Fall - ing   on   the   play - ground.

When   we   hear   it   in   the   house,

We   hear   a   pit - ter   pat   sound.

Second Lesson

————————————

Here is another song in which "do" and the whole scale have moved.

First, we must be sure we know the rhythm of the notes and rests. Clap the notes and say how fast they go. . . .

What do we call the four signs in the key signature? (Flats) In this song, "do" is in the second space and is the first note. What is the second note? (Re) Sing the notes of the first line. . . .

What is the first note of the second line? (Ti) Sing the names of the notes of the second line while I point to them. . . . Sing the second line while I point to the notes. . . .

Is the third line the same as or similar to any other line? (It is similar to the first line but has notes instead of rests.) Sing the third line of notes. . . .

What are the first two notes of the last line? (Mi so") Sing "mi so." . . . Sing the notes of the last line. . . .

Sing the notes of the whole song. . . .

Sing the song with words. . . .

————————————

ADDITIONAL INFORMATION

The foregoing lessons in reading song music give a basis for figuring out the sounds and rhythms of almost any song. Other notes with different time values and other key signatures will be found in song books. For those who wish to broaden their study, here is a chart of the more common notes and rests. The quarter note is the counting unit.

Note	Rest	Name	Rate of Speed	Time Value
♬♬	⅞	Sixteenth	Fast run	Four notes to a beat
♫	⅞	Eighth	Run	Two notes to a beat
♩	⅞	Quarter	Walk	One beat
♩	—	Half	Slow walk	Two beats
♩.	—	Dotted Half	Slow slow walk	Three beats
o	—	Whole	Ve-ry slow walk	Four beats

Uneven rhythms often encountered include the dotted quarter and eighth (♩. ♪) and the dotted eighth and sixteenth(♪. ♬). Notes with dots after them are held half again as long as plain notes. In songs like "America" and "Jingle Bells," one finds examples of these uneven rhythms.

My   coun - try   'tis   of   thee

Jin - gle   all   the   way.

To read song music which has other key signatures, you should first locate "do" in that key. If the signature contains sharps, the position of the sharp farthest to the right is the position of "ti" in the scale, and the note one place higher (or seven places down) is "do." When the key signature contains flats, the flat farthest to the right is in the position of "fa" in that scale, and one has only to figure up or down from there to find "do."

Because music reading must be done in a required rhythm, it is very important that drill be used as a technique of learning. Your school song books can provide material for extending the study which these lessons have started. Children who can read music will have a tool which they will find useful for all of their lives.

Chapter 4

YOU CAN TEACH SONGS
WITH ACCOMPANIMENT

If you have never accompanied singing, you have no idea of the satisfaction and pleasure awaiting you. It is not necessary or advisable to accompany all songs, and in some cases, an instrumental accompaniment may add a harsh and overbearing sound. But there are many songs which are greatly enhanced by the addition of harmony, and singers will respond by singing more confidently when there is an accompaniment to strengthen and support their voices.

Playing accompaniments for the songs in this chapter is easier than you might think, and I urge you to try the directions I have outlined.

The Piano

Locating Notes on the Piano

The piano keyboard consists of a set of level black and white keys. It is the black keys on which everyone who plays the piano depends to determine one note from the other. You will notice that they are grouped in twos and threes up and down the keyboard.

The notes for instruments are named for the first seven letters of the alphabet—A B C D E F and G. The most useful of these for a piano player is probably C, because when playing a scale from one C to the next, only white keys are used. If a person at the piano started a scale on any other key, he would soon discover that it would be necessary to use at least one black key to make it sound right, and using black keys complicates the job of piano playing.

111

To locate "middle C," sit in front of the piano keyboard as near the middle as possible. Find the group of two black notes closest to the center section. The white note which is adjacent to and directly left of these is middle C. There are usually eight C's on a piano, and all are in the same relationship to the groups of two black notes. To play a C scale, start on C and play the seven notes to the right of it one after the other—C D E F G A B and C.

Playing Chords on the White Keys of the Piano

The rule for constructing a simple chord is to start with the basic note, add the third note above it plus the third note above that one. To play the chord of C, play middle C with the thumb of your right hand, E above that with your third finger, and G above with your fifth finger. Curve the fingers as much as possible over the keyboard. To strike the chord, raise the hand a little above the keys and depress all three simultaneously.

Using the above rule, you can make two other chords which require white keys only. With your hand in the same position play an F chord using F, A and C. Play a G chord using G, B and D.

Now turn to "Songs Using One Chord" further on in this chapter. Choose a song which you know. Play the "First note." This is where you will pitch your voice for the first word. Play the chord rhythmically as you sing the song. Then go on to the following section.

Enriching the Piano Accompaniment

By adding a single note played by the left hand every time you play a chord with the right, you will enrich the sound.

Continue to use the song which you accompanied in the section above and which required one chord of harmony. Find the chord's basic note with your left hand an octave (eight notes) below the note you were playing with your right thumb. While you sing the song, play both hands together—the chord with your right hand and the low note with your left.

Look again at the page with the words of the song you are accompanying. Find the word "Piano." Beside this word will appear the letters "L" which stands for "Left hand" and "R" which stands for "Right hand." See what the first letter is. If it is "L," you will start your accompaniment with the single left hand note; if it is "R," you will start with the right hand chord. For example, beside "Piano" in "Are You Sleeping?" are the letters "L-R." This means that you would play left, right, left, right, back and forth for the duration of the song. "Taps," on the other hand, is marked "R-L-R-R." You would start this song with your right hand playing the chord, the left hand playing its note, then the right hand twice again plus once more (you start over again), then left, right, right, right, left, right, right throughout the song.

Playing Chords on Both Black and White Keys

As soon as your playing requires the use of black keys in addition to white, your task becomes more involved. However, it would be difficult, if not impossible, to sing all songs in the key of C, the key of all white notes, and you must plan to occasionally change keys and use black notes.

There are two keys using one black note each which are relatively easy to play in. The key of F requires the use of Bb, the black note immediately to the left of B. In two-chord songs, you would need the F chord (which you know) and the C₇ chord.

You already know the C chord. The "7" in "C₇" stands for the seventh tone up from the note C. This note must be added to the C chord. In the key of F, the seventh tone up from C would be Bb. To play a C₇ chord, place your right thumb on C, index finger on E, third finger on G, and fifth finger on Bb.

Turn to "Songs Using Two Chords" which is further on in the chapter. Choose a song which you know that requires the chords F and C₇. Check beside the word "Piano" to see the order in which you will use your hands. The chords to be used are written above the words. For example, suppose the first chord is F and the order of hands is "L-R-R." You would start with the left hand playing F and the right hand playing the F chord twice. You would then continue to play left, right, right for every chord written over the words throughout the song. Practice this first. Then sound the first note for singing. Sing (or have someone else sing) while you play the accompaniment.

The key of G is the other key which requires the use of only one black note. This is F# which is the black note immediately to the right of F. The chords you will need for two-chord songs in this key are G (which you know) and D₇. The D₇ chord consists of D which is played by the thumb, F# played by the index finger, A played by the middle finger, and C by the fifth finger.

When playing with two chords in the key of C, you will need to know how to construct a G₇ chord. This should not give you much trouble and should include the notes G B D and F.

Songs which have three chords in the accompaniment will have the above chords plus the following: in the key of C, the F chord; in the key of F, the Bb chord; in the key of G, the C chord. The only chord not familiar to you will be the Bb chord. To play it, use your thumb on Bb, middle finger on D and fifth on F.

Varying the Piano Accompaniment

Once you have mastered the techniques outlined above, you might like to experiment by varying the methods of playing chords to make them sound more interesting. One method would be to invert the chord you play with your right hand. For example, you are required to play the G chord in "Taps." Instead of playing G-B-D in that order, play B below middle C with your thumb, the next D with your second (or third) finger, and G with your fifth finger. The other inversion of the G chord would be constructed with D above middle C played with your thumb, G played with the third finger, and B with the fifth.

Left hand notes can also be varied. In "Taps," your left hand plays G, the basic note of the G chord. But the chord has two other notes which would sound acceptable if used occasionally. For instance, on the word "rest" in the last line of the song, play a low D and play the G below that on "nigh." With practice, you will make choices among the chord notes and develop your own style of playing.

The Autoharp

Advantages of the Autoharp

The name "Autoharp" implies that this instrument is in some way automatic and that it is a harp. The Autoharp resembles a zither and is automatic to the extent that little effort is needed to play one. A dozen or so wooden bars, each representing a different chord, are positioned across the strings. On the undersides of each bar are heavy pieces of felt between which are spaces wide enough to accommodate single strings. When a bar is pressed and the strings are strummed or made to vibrate, the felts prevent unwanted strings from sounding and permit unblocked strings to vibrate.

The Autoharp is a harmonizing instrument. A first grade child can play accompaniments for one-chord songs, and children from second grade on can learn to accompany songs that require two chords. However, it takes time to train young children, and, in the lower grades at least, it will probably be more expedient if the better part of the accompanying is done by the teacher.

Not only is the Autoharp easy to play; its tones blend well with singing voices. Also in its favor is its portability. It is a lightweight instrument that takes up little space. Another reason to consider the Autoharp is that most song books have Autoharp chord letters written over the words of a great many songs.

An Autoharp is not expensive. If you are considering purchasing one, I recommend that you select one with at least twelve chord bars, partly because the strings are longer and therefore the tone is better than that of a smaller-sized instrument, and partly because you will be able to accompany more songs with the additional bars.

Tuning the Autoharp

Before you start to play a new Autoharp, it will have to be tuned. If your music teacher or consultant cannot assist you, you may have to tune it yourself. Once it has been tuned, you will find that every few weeks or so, it may become noticeably out of tune. The need to tune it will vary with the season of the year and with changes in the atmosphere, especially changes in heat and moisture which are responsible for the expansion and contraction of wood and strings and for the loosening of the pins which hold the strings.

Take your Autoharp with the tuning key to a piano. Place it on your lap with the long side next to you. Slip the tuning key over the pin nearest to you to which the first long string is attached. Play the corresponding note of the string on the piano (probably it will be a low F). Then pick the string. If it sounds lower than the piano note, tighten the pin with the key, turning it slowly. Again play the note on the piano and again pick the string and again tighten the pin if necessary. Repeat the process until the string of the Autoharp is on pitch.

Slip the tuning key onto the next pin. Notice the note name of that string, because it may not be the next note of the scale. Autoharp notes do not follow a scale sequence. Some will be sharped and some flatted. When finding these on the piano, remember that a note with a sharp (♯) will be the black note immediately to the right of the note named, and a note with a flat (♭) is the black note adjacent to and to the left of the note named.

Tune every string in sequence. Then test the Autoharp by playing every chord. If you hear any chords that sound out of tune, try to remember the notes included in those chords (or, better yet, write the notes down). Suppose the D_7 and the C chords sound off key. The notes in the D_7 chord would be D, F♯, A, and C and in the C chord C, E, and G. Since both chords contain C, there is a likelihood that a C string may be at fault. Check all C's first, and try the chords again. If a chord still sounds discordant, you will have to check the notes of that chord.

When your Autoharp sounds out of tune, do not plan to tune every string. Strum the chords and remember or write down the notes in chords that sound wrong and check only the strings involved.

Playing the Autoharp

The Autoharp may be held on your lap or placed on a table with the chord letters facing you. Turn to "Songs Using One Chord" and choose a song familiar to you. Find the button of the chord listed for the song, and press it firmly with the index finger of your left hand. Now cross your right hand over your left, and with a pick (or with the index finger of your right hand), strum across the entire range of strings, moving away from your body. Strum rhythmically as you sing the song.

Now turn to "Songs Using Two Chords" and find a song you know how to sing. Find the buttons of the two chords listed and place the index finger of your left hand over the button further to the right and the third finger (or whichever is comfortable) over the second button. Look at the first word with a chord letter over it and depress the appropriate button. If necessary, pluck the string of the "First note" to get the starting pitch. (Usually you can sense the sound of the first note by listening to the first chord.) As you play the accompaniment, sing the song, watching the letters over the words for chord changes. Do not attempt songs using three chords until you have had a lot of practice with one- and two-chord songs.

When accompanying songs using two or more chords, always keep the fingers that will be needed directly over the buttons of the chord bars, ready to use. If a chord is repeated, do not raise the finger holding the chord bar between strums. If your playing sounds blurred, press the chord bar more firmly.

A substantial number of songs in this book will be known to you and will provide you with a good beginning repertoire. Songs in the children's texts which have chord letters over the words will allow you to extend your ability to accompany on the Autoharp.

THE SONGS

Songs Using One Chord

RING AROUND A ROSY   Grades 1, 2

   First note: G   *Piano:* L-R   *Chord:* C
   Ring around a rosy,   A pocket full of posey,
   Hop scotch, hop scotch,   And all fall down.

ARE YOU SLEEPING? (FRÈRE JACQUES) (Traditional)
                                                         Grades 1-6

   First note: F   *Piano:* L-R   *Chord:* F
   Are you sleeping?   Are you sleeping?
   Brother John,   Brother John,
   Morning bells are ringing,   Morning bells are ringing,
   Ding, ding, dong,   Ding, ding, dong.

ROW, ROW, ROW YOUR BOAT (Old Round)   Grades 1-6

   First note: C   *Piano:* L-R   *Chord:* C
   Row, row, row your boat   Gently down the stream,
   Merrily, merrily, merrily, merrily,   Life is but a dream.

TAPS (U.S. Army Bugle Call)   Grades 2-6

First note: D   *Piano:* R-L-R-R   *Chord:* G
Day is done,   Gone the sun
From the lake, from the hills, from the sky;
All is well,   Safely rest,   God is nigh.

LOVELY EVENING (Round)   Grades 3-6

First note: F   *Piano:* L-R-R   *Chord:* F
Oh, how lovely is the evening, is the evening,
When the bells are sweetly ringing, sweetly ringing,
Ding, dong, ding, dong, ding, dong.

THE LONE STAR TRAIL (American Cowboy Song)   Grades 3-6

First note: C   *Piano:* R-L-R-R   *Chord:* F
1. I started on the trail on June twenty-third.
   I been punching Texas cattle on the Lone Star Trail,
Refrain: Singing ki-yi yippy yappy yay, yappy yay,
   Singing ki-yi yippy yappy yay.
2. It's cloudy in the west, a-lookin' like rain,
   A-and my old slicker's in the wagon again,
        (Refrain)

Songs Using Two Chords

THE FARMER IN THE DELL (Singing Game)   Grades 1, 2

First note: low C   *Piano:* L-R   *Chords:* F C₇

| | F | | F | | F | | F |
1. The farmer in the dell,   The farmer in the dell,

| | F | | F | | C₇ | | F |
Heigh-ho, the derry-o,   The farmer in the dell.
2. The farmer takes a wife. . . .
3. The wife takes a child. . . .
4. The child takes a dog. . . .
5. The dog takes a cat. . . .
6. The cat takes the mouse. . . .
7. The mouse takes the cheese. . . .
8. The cheese stands alone. . . .

LONDON BRIDGE (Singing Game)   Grades 1, 2

First note: high C   *Piano:* L-R   *Chords:* F C₇

| | F | | F | | C₇ | | F |
1. London bridge is falling down, falling down, falling down,

| | F | | F | | C₇ | | F |
London bridge is falling down,   My fair lady.

2. Build it up with iron bars. . . .
3. Iron bars will rust and break. . . .
4. Build it up with sticks and stones. . . .
5. Sticks and stones will soon fall down. . . .

EENCY WEENCY SPIDER (Traditional) Grades 1, 2

First note: low C   *Piano:* L-R   *Chords:* F C$_7$

F   F   C$_7$ F
An eency weency spider went up the water spout,
F   F   C$_7$ F
Down came the rain and washed the spider out.
F   F   C$_7$ F
Out came the sun and dried up all the rain,
F   F   C$_7$ F
And the eency weency spider went up the spout again.

MULBERRY BUSH (Traditional Singing Game) Grades 1, 2

First note: G   *Piano:* L-R   *Chords:* G D$_7$

G   G
1. Here we go round the mulberry bush,
      D$_7$ D$_7$
The mulberry bush, the mulberry bush,
G   G
Here we go round the mulberry bush,
      D$_7$ G
So early in the morning.

2. This is the way we wash our clothes. . . .
3. This is the way we iron our clothes. . . .
4. This is the way we clap our hands. . . .
5. This is the way we march in place. . . . etc.

MARY HAD A LITTLE LAMB (Traditional) Grades 1, 2

First note: A   *Piano:* L-R   *Chords:* F C$_7$

F   F   C$_7$ F
1. Mary had a little lamb, Little lamb, little lamb,
F   F   C$_7$ F
Mary had a little lamb, Its fleece was white as snow.
2. Everywhere that Mary went, . . . The lamb was sure to go.
3. It followed her to school one day, . . . Which was against
                       the rule.
4. It made the children laugh and shout, . . . To see a lamb
                       at school.

DID YOU EVER SEE A LASSIE? (Traditional) Grades 1, 2

First note: F   *Piano:* L-R-R   *Chords:* F C$_7$

<pre>
         F   F   C₇   F
</pre>
1. Did you ever see a lassie, a lassie, a lassie,
<pre>
         F   F   C₇   F
</pre>
   Did you ever see a lassie, go this way and that?
<pre>
   C₇   F   C₇   F
</pre>
   Go this way and that way, go this way and that way?
<pre>
         F   F   C⁷   F
</pre>
   Did you ever see a lassie go this way and that?
2. Did you ever see a laddie. . . .

JOHN BROWN HAD A LITTLE INDIAN (Traditional) Grades 1, 2

First note: G   *Piano:* L-R   *Chords:* G D₇

<pre>
   G   G
</pre>
1. John Brown had a little Indian,
<pre>
   D₇   D₇
</pre>
   John Brown had a little Indian,
<pre>
   G   G
</pre>
   John Brown had a little Indian,
<pre>
   D₇   G
</pre>
   One little Indian boy.

2. One little, two little, three little Indians,
   Four little, five little, six little Indians,
   Seven little, eight little, nine little Indians,
   Ten little Indian boys.

3. Ten little, nine little, eight little Indians,
   Seven little, six little, five little Indians,
   Four little, three little, two little Indians,
   One little Indian boy.

WHERE HAS MY LITTLE DOG GONE? (Traditional)

Grades 1-3

First note: A   *Piano:* L-R-R   *Chords:* F C₇
<pre>
   F   F   C₇   C₇
</pre>
Oh, where, oh, where has my little dog gone?
<pre>
   C₇   C₇   F   F
</pre>
Oh, where, oh, where can he be?
<pre>
         F   F   C₇   C₇
</pre>
With his ears cut short and his tail cut long,
<pre>
   C₇   C₇   F
</pre>
Oh, where, oh, where can he be?

PAWPAW PATCH (American Singing Game)

Grades 1-3

First note: F   *Piano:* L-R   *Chords:* F C₇
<pre>
   F   F
</pre>
1. Where, O where is dear little Jenny,

C₇   C₇
Where, O where is dear little Jenny,
F   F
Where, O where is dear little Jenny?
C₇   F
'Way down yonder in the pawpaw patch.

2. Pickin' up pawpaws, puttin' 'em in a basket. . . .
3. Come on, boys, and let's go find her. . . .
4. Here she comes and we'll go with her. . . .

HOT CROSS BUNS (Traditional)   Grades 1-3

First note: A   *Piano:* Both hands   *Chords:* F C₇

F   C₇   F   F   C₇   F
Hot cross buns,   Hot cross buns,
F   F   C₇   C₇   F   C₇   F
One a penny, two a penny,   Hot cross buns.

DOWN BY THE STATION (Traditional)   Grades 1-3

First note: G   *Piano:* L-R   *Chords:* G D₇

G   G   D₇   G
Down by the station early in the morning,
G   G   D₇   G
See the little pufferbillies all in a row.
G   G   D₇   G
See the little driver pull the little handle.
G   G   D₇   G
Puff, puff! Choo, choo! Off they go!

THREE BLIND MICE (Round)   Grades 1-4

First note: E   *Piano:* Both hands   *Chords:* C G₇

C   G₇   C - C   G₇   C -
Three blind mice,   Three blind mice,
C   G₇   C - C   G₇   C -
See how they run!   See how they run!
C   G₇   C   -   C   G₇
They all ran after the farmer's wife, She cut off their tails
C   -
with a carving knife,
C   G₇   C   -   C   G₇   C
Did you ever see such a sight in your life As three blind mice?

GO TELL AUNT RHODIE (American Folk Song)   Grades 1-4

First note: A   *Piano:* L-R   *Chords:* F C₇

F   F   C₇   F
1. Go tell Aunt Rhodie,   Go tell Aunt Rhodie,
F   F   C₇   F
Go tell Aunt Rhodie,   Her old gray goose is dead.

2. The one she'd been saving. . . . To make a feather bed.
3. She died in the mill pond. . . . Standing on her head.
4. The goslings are crying. . . . The old gray goose is dead.
5. The gander is weeping. . . . The old gray goose is dead.

HUSH, LITTLE BABY (Southern Folk Song)   Grades 1-4

First note: D   *Piano:* L-R-R-R   *Chords:* G D$_7$

   G   D$_7$
1. Hush, little baby, don't say a word,
   D$_7$ G
   Papa's going to buy you a mocking bird.
2. If that mocking bird won't sing,
   Papa's going to buy you a diamond ring.
3. If that diamond ring turns brass,
   Papa's going to buy you a looking glass.
4. If that looking glass gets broke,
   Papa's going to buy you a billy goat.
5. If that billy goat won't pull,
   Papa's going to buy you a cart and bull.
6. If that cart and bull turn over,
   Papa's going to buy you a dog named Rover.
7. If that dog named Rover won't bark,
   Papa's going to buy you a horse and cart.
8. If that horse and cart break down,
   We'll take a walk all around the town.

THE MORE WE GET TOGETHER (German Folk Song)

Grades 1-6

First note: F   *Piano:* L-R-R   *Chords:* F C$_7$
   F   F   C$_7$ F
The more we get together, together, together,
   F   F   C$_7$ F
The more we get together, the happier we'll be.
   C$_7$ F   C$_7$ F
For your friends are my friends, and my friends are your friends,
   F   F   C$_7$ F
The more we get together, the happier we'll be.

POLLY WOLLY DOODLE (American Folk Song)   Grades 1-6

First note: F   *Piano:* L-R-R-R   *Chords:* F C$_7$
   F   F
1. Oh, I went down South to see my Sal,
   F   C$_7$
   Sing Polly wolly doodle all the day;
   C$_7$ C$_7$
   My Sally is a spunky gal

      C₇   F
Sing Polly wolly doodle all the day.
              F   F
Refrain: Fare thee well, fare thee well,
         F   C₇
Fare thee well my fairy fay,
      C₇   C₇
For I'm going to Louisiana, for to see my Susyanna,
      C₇   F
Sing Polly wolly doodle all the day.

2. My Sally is a maiden fair, Sing. . . .
   With curly eyes and laughing hair, Sing. . . .
                (Refrain)

3. Behind the barn, down on my knees, Sing. . . .
   I thought I heard a chicken sneeze, Sing. . . .
                (Refrain)

4. He sneezed so hard with whoopin' cough, Sing. . . .
   He sneezed his head and tail right off, Sing. . . .
                (Refrain)

DOWN IN THE VALLEY (American Folk Song)   Grades 1-6

First note: D   *Piano:* L-R-R   *Chords:* G D₇

     D₇   G G   G   D₇ D₇
1. Down in the valley, the valley so low,
     D₇   D₇ D₇ D₇   G G
   Hang your head over, hear the wind blow.
     D₇   G   G   G   D₇ D₇
   Hear the wind blow, dear, hear the wind blow,
     D₇   D₇ D₇ D₇   G G
   Hang your head over, hear the wind blow.

2. Writing this letter, containing three lines,
   Answer my question, "Will you be mine?"
   "Will you be mine, dear, will you be mine?"
   Answer my question, "Will you be mine?"

3. Build me a castle forty feet high,
   So I can see him as he goes by.
   As he goes by, dear, as he goes by,
   So I can see him as he goes by.

4. Roses love sunshine, violets love dew,
   Angels in heaven know I love you.
   Know I love you, dear, know I love you,
   Angels in heaven know I love you.

HE'S GOT THE WHOLE WORLD IN HIS HANDS (Spiritual)

Grades 1-6

First note: G   *Piano:* L-R-R-R   *Chords:* C G$_7$

    C   C
1. He's got the whole world in His hands,
    G$_7$ G$_7$
    He's got the whole world in His hands,
    C   C
    He's got the whole world in His hands,
    G$_7$ C
    He's got the whole world in His hands.
2. He's got the little bitty baby. . . .
3. He's got you and me, brother. . . .
4. He's got the wind and the rain. . . .

RIG-A-JIG-JIG (English Folk Song)

Grades 1-6

First note: G   *Piano:* L-R   *Chords:* C G$_7$

    C   C
As I was walking down the street,
    G$_7$ C
Heigh-o, heigh-o, heigh-o, heigh-o,
    C   C
A pretty girl I chanced to meet,
    G$_7$ C
Heigh-o, heigh-o, heigh-o.
    C   C
Rig-a-jig-jig and away we go,
    G$_7$ C
Away we go, away we go;
    C   C
Rig-a-jig-jig and away we go,
    G$_7$ C
Heigh-o, heigh-o, heigh-o.

LEAVIN' OLD TEXAS (Cowboy Song)

Grades 3-6

First note: low C   *Piano:* L-R-R-R   *Chords:* F C$_7$

    F   F
1. I'm goin' to leave/Old Texas now,
    C$_7$ F
    They've got no use/For the long-horned cow.
2. They've plowed and fenced/My cattle range,
    And the people there/Are all so strange.
3. I'll bid adios/To the Alamo,
    And set my face/Toward Mexico.

124 YOU CAN TEACH SONGS WITH ACCOMPANIMENT

4. The hard, hard ground/Will be my bed,
And the saddle seat/Will hold my head.
5. And when I waken/From my dreams,
I'll eat my bread/And my sardines.

LONG, LONG AGO (Thomas H. Bayley)   Grades 4-6

First note: F   *Piano:* L-R   *Chords:* F C₇

  F   F   F   F
Tell me the tales that to me were so dear,
 C₇   C₇ C₇   F
Long, long ago, long, long ago;
 F   F   F   F
Sing me the songs I delighted to hear,
 C₇   C₇   F
Long, long ago, long ago.

JOSHUA FIT THE BATTLE OF JERICHO (Negro Folk Song)

Grades 4-6

First note: D   (Autoharp only)   *Chords:* D min A₇

    D min.   D min.
Refrain: Joshua fit the battle of Jericho,
   A₇   D min.
Jericho, Jericho,
D min.   D min.
Joshua fit the battle of Jericho,
      A₇   D min.
And the walls came tumbling down.

      D min.   D min.
Verse: You may talk about your kings of Gideon,
     D min.   A₇
You may talk about your men of Saul
     D min.   D min.
But there's none like good old Joshua
   A₇   D min.
At the battle of Jericho.   (Refrain)

CLEMENTINE (Percy Montrose)   Grades 4-6

First note: F   *Piano:* L-R-R   *Chords:* F C₇

  F   F   F   C₇
1. In a cavern, in a canyon, Excavating for a mine
      C₇   F   C₇   F
Dwelt a miner, forty niner, And his daughter, Clementine.
            F   F   F
Refrain: Oh, my darling, Oh, my darling, Oh, my darling Clem-
          C₇
entine,

       C₇   F   C₇   F

You are lost and gone forever, Dreadful sorry, Clementine.

2. Light she was and like a feather, And her shoes were number
                                  nine,
   Herring boxes without topses, Sandals were for Clementine.
                  (Refrain)

3. Drove she ducklings to the water, Every morning just at nine,
   Hit her foot against a splinter, Fell into the foaming brine.
                  (Refrain)

For other songs in this book using two chords, see:

   LOOBY LOO, p. 46
   SHOO, FLY, DON'T BOTHER ME, p. 49
   CHRISTMAS DANCE, p. 54
   HAWAIIAN BOAT SONG, p. 57
   CSHEBOGAR, p. 62
   MEXICAN HAT DANCE, p. 71

Songs Using Three Chords

I'M A LITTLE TEAPOT (Traditional)   Grades 1-2

   First note: low C   *Piano:* L-R   *Chords:* C G₇ F
   C   C   F   C
   I'm a little teapot, short and stout;
   G₇   C   G₇   C
   Here is my handle, here is my spout.
   C   C   F   C
   When I get all steamed up, then I shout,
   C   F   G₇   C
   Just tip me over and pour me out!

THE MUFFIN MAN (Traditional English)   Grades 1-2

   First note: D   *Piano:* L-R-R-R   *Chords:* G D₇ C
   G   G
  1. Oh, do you know the muffin man,
      C   D₇
   The muffin man, the muffin man?
     G   G
   Oh, do you know the muffin man
      C   D₇   G
   That lives in Drury Lane?
  2. Oh, yes I know the muffin man. . . .

HICKORY DICKORY DOCK (J. W. Elliot)   Grades 1-2

   First note: A   *Piano:* Both hands   *Chords:* F C₇ B♭

　　　　F　　C₇　　F　　　　F　　　C₇　　　F
Hickory dickory dock,/The mouse ran up the clock;
　　　　F　　　　F　　　B♭　　　B♭　　C₇　　C₇　　F
The clock struck one, the mouse ran down,/Hickory dickory dock.

TWINKLE, TWINKLE, LITTLE STAR (Traditional)　　Grades 1-3

First note: F　　　　　　*Piano:* L-R　　　　*Chords:* F C₇ B♭

　　　　F　　　F　　　B♭　　F
Twinkle, twinkle, little star,
　　　　C₇　　　F　　C₇　　　　F
How I wonder what you are!
　　　　F　C₇　　　F　　　C₇
Up above the world so high,
　　　　F　　　C₇　　F　　　C₇
Like a diamond in the sky;
　　　　F　　　F　　　B♭　　F
Twinkle, twinkle, little star,
　　　　C₇　　　F　　C₇　　　　F
How I wonder what you are!

OLD MACDONALD HAD A FARM (Traditional)　　　Grades 1-3

First note: G　　　　　*Piano:* L-R　　　　*Chords:* G D₇ C

　　　　G　　　G　　　C　　G G　　　D₇　　　G G
1. Old MacDonald had a farm, E—I—E—I—O!
　　　　　　G　　　G　　　C　　　G G　　　D₇　　　G G
And on this farm he had some chicks, E—I—E—I—O!
　　　　　　G　　　　G　　　　G　　　　　G
With a chick, chick here, and a chick, chick there,
　　　　G　　　C　　　　G　　　　C
Here a chick, there a chick, ev'rywhere a chick, chick,
　　　　G　　　G　　C　　G G　　　D₇　　G
Old MacDonald had a farm, E—I—E—I—O!
2. . . .some ducks . . . (quack, quack)
3. . . .some turkeys . . . (gobble, gobble)
4. . . .some pigs . . . (oink, oink)
5. . . .a truck . . . (rattle, rattle)

UP ON THE HOUSE-TOP (Traditional)　　　　Grades 1-3

First note: high C　　　*Piano:* L-R　　　*Chords:* F C₇ B♭

　　　　F　　　　F　　　　　F　　　F
1. Up on the house-top the reindeer pause,
　　　　B♭　　　F　　　C₇　　C₇
Out jumps good old Santa Claus;
　　　　F　　　　　F　　　F　　F
Down through the chimney with lots of toys,
　　B♭　　　F　　　C₇　　F
All for the little ones' Christmas joys.

```
        Bb       Bb    F              F
Refrain: Ho, ho, ho! Who wouldn't go!
        C₇       C₇    F              F
Ho, ho, ho! Who wouldn't go-o!
        F        F     Bb             Bb
Up on the house-top, click, click, click,
        F        F     C₇             F
Down through the chimney with good Saint Nick.
```

2. First comes the stocking of little Nell;
   Oh, dear Santa, fill it well;
   Give her a dolly that laughs and cries,
   One that can open and shut its eyes.
                    (Refrain)

OATS AND BEANS AND BARLEY GROW (English Singing Game)
Grades 1-3

First note: B   (Autoharp only)   *Chords:* G A min. D₇
```
    G          G          G    G
1. Oats and beans and barley grow,
   A min.   A min.      D₇   D₇
   Oats and beans and barley grow,
    G    D₇   G     G
   Can you or I or anyone know
     A min.   D₇        G    G
   How oats and beans and barley grow?
```

2. Thus the farmer sows his seed,
   Thus he stands and takes his ease;
   He stamps his foot and claps his hands
   And turns around to view the land.

3. Waiting for a partner,
   Waiting for a partner,
   Open the ring and choose one in
   While we all gaily dance and sing.

BINGO (American Folk Song)
Grades 1-4

First note: low D   *Piano:* L-R   *Chords:* G D₇ C
```
        G     G    C   G      G   D₇     G  G
There was a farmer had a dog, And Bingo was his name-O.
G   G  C      C   D₇ D₇  G     G
B—I—N—G—O,  B—I—N—G—O,
G   G  C      C        D₇  D₇     G  G
B—I—N—G—O,   And Bingo was his name-O.
```

THIS OLD MAN (English Children's Song)
Grades 1-4

First note: high C   *Piano:* L-R   *Chords:* F C₇ Bb

```
       F      F   F          F
1. This old man, he played one,
   Bb        Bb      C7       C7
   He played nick-nack on my thumb,
              F       F       Bb          F
   With a nick-nack, paddy whack, give a dog a bone,
   C7      C7       F    F
   This old man came rolling home.
```

2. . . .two . . . shoe
3. . . .three . . . knee
4. . . .four . . . door
5. . . .five . . . hive
6. . . .six . . . sticks
7. . . .seven . . . up in heaven
8. . . .eight . . . gate
9. . . .nine . . . spine
10. . . .ten . . . once again.

SHE'LL BE COMIN' 'ROUND THE MOUNTAIN (American Folk Song)   Grades 1-4

First note: low D   *Piano:* L-R-R-R   *Chords:* G D7 C

```
                      G                                    G
1. She'll be comin' 'round the mountain when she comes,
                      G                                    D7
   She'll be comin' 'round the mountain when she comes,
                      G                                    C
   She'll be comin' 'round the mountain, she'll be comin'
                              'round the mountain,
                      D7                               G
   She'll be comin' 'round the mountain when she comes.
```

2. She'll be drivin' six white horses. . . .
3. We will all go down to meet her. . . .
4. We will kill the old red rooster. . . .
5. We will all have chicken 'n' dumplings. . . .

YANKEE DOODLE (Traditional)   Grades 1-4

First note: G   *Piano:* L-R   *Chords:* G D7 C

```
   G     G    G     D7
1. Yankee Doodle came to town,
   G     G   G D7
   Riding on a pony;
   G      G    C     C
   Stuck a feather in his cap
        D7   D7   G  G
   And called it Macaroni.
```

          C   C   C   C
Refrain: Yankee Doodle keep it up,
      G   G   G G
     Yankee Doodle dandy,
       C   C   C   C
     Mind the music and the step
        G D_7 G G
     And with the girls be handy.

2. Fath'r and I went down to camp,
   Along with Captain Goodwin,
   And there we saw the men and boys
   As thick as hasty pudding.
      (Refrain)

3. There was Captain Washington
   Upon a slapping stallion,
   A-giving orders to his men;
   I guess there was a million.
      (Refrain)

MAN ON THE FLYING TRAPEZE (Traditional)   Grades 1-6

First note: low D   *Piano:* L-R-R   *Chords:* G D_7 C

   G   G   C   C
He flies through the air with the greatest of ease,
   D_7 D_7 G   G
This daring young man on the flying trapeze,
   G   G   C   C
His actions are graceful, all girls he does please,
   D_7 D_7 G
And my love he has stolen away.

AMERICA (Henry Carey)   Grades 1-6

First note: F   *Piano:* L-R-R   *Chords:* F C_7 B♭

 F C_7
My country, 'tis of thee,
 F   F
Sweet land of liberty,
C_7 F
Of thee I sing;
 F   F
Land where my fathers died,
C_7 C_7
Land of the Pilgrim's pride,
F   F
From ev'ry mountain side
B♭ (F C_7) F
Let freedom ring!

OH, SUSANNA (S. Foster)   Grades 1-6

First note: F   *Piano:* L-R   *Chords:* F C₇ B♭

  F   F F F   F F   C₇ C₇

1. I came from Alabama with my banjo on my knee,

  F   F F F F   C₇   F

I'm going to Louisiana, my true love for to see.

  F   F   F F   F   F   C₇ C₇

It rained all night the day I left, the weather it was dry,

  F   F F F   F   C₇   F

The sun so hot I froze to death; Susanna, don't you cry.

  B♭ B♭ B♭ B♭   F   F   C₇ C₇

Refrain: Oh, Susanna! Oh, don't you cry for me,

  F   F F F   F   C₇   F

I've come from Alabama with my banjo on my knee.

2. I had a dream the other night, when ev'rything was still;
I throught I saw Susanna, a-coming down the hill;
The buckwheat cake was in her mouth, the tear was in her eye;
Says I, I'm coming from the South, Susanna, don't you cry.
(Refrain)

FOR HE'S A JOLLY GOOD FELLOW (Traditional)   Grades 1-6

First note: F   *Piano:* L-R   *Chords:* F C₇ B♭

  F   F   C₇   F

1. For he's a jolly good fellow, for he's a jolly good fellow,

  F   B♭   C₇   F

For he's a jolly good fellow, which nobody can deny.

  F (B♭) F   F (B♭) F

Which nobody can deny, which nobody can deny.
(Repeat first two lines.)

2. The bear went over the mountain . . . to see what he could see!
And all that he could see. . . .
Was the other side of the mountain . . . was all that he
could see!

LAVENDER'S BLUE (English Folk Song)   Grades 1-6

First note: G   *Piano:* L-R-R   *Chords:* C F G

 C   C   F   C

Lavender's blue, dilly dilly, Lavender's green.

 C   C   G   G

When I am king, dilly dilly, You shall be queen.

 C   C   F   C

Who told you so, dilly dilly, Who told you so?

 F   C   G   C

'Twas my own heart, dilly dilly, That told me so.

O CHRISTMAS TREE (German Folk Song)   Grades 1-6

First note: low C   *Piano:* L-R-R   *Chords:* F C₇ B♭

     F   (C₇)   F
O Christmas tree, O Christmas tree,
     B♭   (C₇)   F
How lovely are thy branches.
    (Repeat)
     F   C₇
Thy boughs so green in summertime
     C₇   F
Will be as green in wintertime.
    (Repeat first two lines.)

SILENT NIGHT (Franz Grüber)   Grades 1-6

First note: G   *Piano:* L-R-R (or both hands) *Chords* C G₇ F

    C   (C)   C   (C)
1. Silent night! Holy night!
    G₇   (G₇)   C   (C)
All is calm, all is bright
    F   (F)   C   (C)
'Round yon virgin mother and Child,
    F (F)   C   (C)
Holy Infant, so tender and mild,
    G₇   (G₇)   C (C)
Sleep in heavenly peace,
    C   (G₇)   C
Sleep in heavenly peace.

2. Silent night! Holy night!
Shepherds quake at the sight,
Glories stream from heaven afar,
Heav'nly hosts sing Alleluia;
Christ, the Savior, is born,
Christ, the Savior, is born.

AWAY IN A MANGER (J. R. Murray)   Grades 1-6

First note: high D   *Piano:* Both hands   *Chords:* G D₇ C

    G   G   C   G
1. Away in a manger, no crib for a bed,
     D₇   D₇   G   G
The little Lord Jesus laid down His sweet head.
     G   G   C   G
The stars in the sky looked down where He lay,
     D₇   G   C   (D₇) G
The little Lord Jesus, asleep in the hay.

2. The cattle are lowing, the poor Baby wakes,

But little Lord Jesus, no crying He makes.
I love Thee, Lord Jesus, look down from the sky,
And stay by my cradle till morning is nigh.

JINGLE BELLS (J. Pierpont)   Grades 1-6

First note: low D   *Piano:* L-R-R-R   *Chords:* G D$_7$ C

G   G   G   C
Dashing through the snow/In a one-horse open sleigh,
C   D$_7$ D$_7$ G
O'er the fields we go,/Laughing all the way;
G   G   G   C
Bells on bob-tail ring,/Making spirits bright,
            C   D$_7$ D$_7$ G
What fun it is to ride and sing/A sleighing song tonight.
            G   G   G   (C)   G
Refrain: Jingle bells, jingle bells,/Jingle all the way.
C   G   D$_7$ D$_7$
Oh, what fun it is to ride/In a one-horse open sleigh.
G   G   G   (C)   G
Jingle bells, jingle bells,/Jingle all the way.
C   G   D$_7$ G
Oh, what fun it is to ride/In a one-horse open sleigh.

CAMPTOWN RACES (Stephen Foster)   Grades 3-6

First note: G   *Piano:* L-R-R-R   *Chords:* C G$_7$ F

        C   C   G$_7$ G$_7$
The Camptown ladies sing this song, Doo-dah, doo-dah!
        C   C   G$_7$ C
The Camptown race track five miles long, Oh, doo-dah day!
        C   C   G$_7$ G$_7$
I come down there with my hat caved in, Doo-dah, doo-dah!
C   C   G$_7$ C
I go back home with a pocket full of tin, Oh, doo-dah day!
C   C   F   C
Going to run all night, Going to run all day.
            C   C   G$_7$ C
I'll bet my money on the bob-tail nag, Somebody bet on the bay.

SWANEE RIVER (Stephen Foster)   Grades 3-6

First note: E   *Piano:* L-R   *Chords:* C G$_7$ F

C G$_7$ C   F
'Way down upon the Swanee River,
C C G$_7$ G$_7$
Far, far away,
        C   G$_7$ C   F
There's where my heart is turning ever,

    C   G₇   C C
   There's where the old folks stay.
   C G₇   C   F
   All up and down the whole creation,
    C C G₇ G₇
   Sadly I roam,
    C G₇   C   F
   Still longing for the old plantation,
    C   G₇   C C
   And for the old folks at home.
   G₇   G₇   C   C
   All the world is sad and dreary,
   F   F   C G₇
   Everywhere I roam;
    C G₇   C   F
   Oh, brothers, how my heart grows weary,
    C   G₇   C
   Far from the old folks at home.

AULD LANG SYNE (Scotch Folk Song)   Grades 3-6

  First note: low C   *Piano:* L-R-R-R *Chords:* F C₇ B♭
     F   C₇
   Should auld acquaintance be forgot,
     F   B♭
   And never brought to mind?
     F   C₇
   Should auld acquaintance be forgot,
    B♭ (C₇)   F
   And days of auld lang syne?
     F   C₇
   For auld lang syne, my dear,
     F   B♭
   For auld lang syne;
     F   C₇
   We'll take a cup o'kindness yet
    B♭ (C₇) F
   For auld lang syne.

HOME ON THE RANGE (Cowboy Song)   Grades 3-6

  First note: low C   *Piano:* L-R-R   *Chords:* F C₇ B♭
    F   F   B♭ B♭
   Oh, give me a home where the buffalo roam,
       F   F   C₇ C₇
   Where the deer and the antelope play;
     F   F   B♭   B♭
   Where seldom is heard a discouraging word,

      F   C₇   F   F

F   C₇   F   F

And the skies are not cloudy all day.

  F   C₇   F   F

Home, home on the range,

         F   F   C₇   C₇

Where the deer and the antelope play;

      F   F   B♭   B♭

Where seldom is heard a discouraging word,

    F   C₇   F

And the skies are not cloudy all day.

SWING LOW, SWEET CHARIOT (Spiritual)   Grades 3-6

First note: A   *Piano:* Both hands   *Chords:* F C₇ B♭

                F   B♭ C₇

Refrain: Swing low, sweet chariot,

  F   C₇

Comin' for to carry me home,

  F   B♭ C₇

Swing low, sweet chariot,

    F   F   C₇ F

Comin' for to carry me home.

    F   F   B♭   C₇

1. I looked over Jordan and what did I see,

  F   C₇

Comin' for to carry me home,

    F   B♭   C₇

A band of angels comin' after me,

  F   C₇ F

Comin' for to carry me home. (Refrain)

2. I'm sometimes up and sometimes down,
   Comin' for to carry me home,
   But still my soul feels heavenly bound,
   Comin' for to carry me home. (Refrain)

GO TELL IT ON THE MOUNTAIN (Spiritual)   Grades 3-6

First note: B   *Piano:* L-R-R-R   *Chords:* G D₇ C

G   G   D₇   G

When I was a seeker, I sought both night and day,

G   G   C   D₇

I asked the Lord to help me, And He showed me the way.

G (C)   G   D₇   G

Go tell it on the mountain, Over the hills and ev'rywhere,

G (C)   G   G (D₇)   G

Go tell it on the mountain That Jesus Christ is born.

RED RIVER VALLEY (American Folk Song)   Grades 3-6

First note: low D   *Piano:* L-R-R-R   *Chords:* G D₇ C

        G   G   C C
From this valley they say you are going,

        G   G   D₇ D₇
We will miss your bright eyes and sweet smile,

        G   G   C C
For they say you are taking the sunshine,

        G   D₇   G
That brightens our pathway awhile.

              G   G   C C
Refrain: Come and sit by my side if you love me,

        G   G   D₇ D₇
Do not hasten to bid me adieu,

        G   G   C C
But remember the Red River Valley,

        G   D₇   G
And the girl that has loved you so true.

For other songs in this book using three chords, see:

OLD BRASS WAGON, p. 51
ACH, JA! p. 56
NORWEGIAN PEASANT DANCE, p. 64
POLKA, p. 67
TURKEY IN THE STRAW, p. 69

Part Three

TEACHING MUSIC

APPRECIATION

Great music endures and remains timely for people of all ages. The music of Brahms, Tchaikovsky, Schumann, and Strauss has survived 100 years. The music of Bach, Handel, Scarlatti, and Vivaldi is being heard and enjoyed 250 years after it was written.

Why do people still love and appreciate the music of these master composers? What qualities are contained in great music that insure its vitality and its durability? Apparently there are elements that symbolize the feelings of people—people of any time and of any place. Great music ennobles and inspires and gives listeners a sense of the dignity of man. People feel a bond of understanding with the men who wrote it, regardless of how long ago this might have been.

Children of all ages are capable of sensing the height of feeling to which great music can lead them. Because they are highly receptive to these sounds, it is most important that schools provide opportunities for them to hear it, study it, and learn to appreciate it.

How can teachers help children appreciate music? Three methods are here recommended. The first is to expose them to the sounds of the music we eventually want them to take an interest in. The second is to give them experiences in making music, singing it, moving with it, and dancing to it. The third is to give them specific training in what to listen for.

Exposing Children to Music

Learning about something by exposure to it is largely a subconscious experience. For example, when two people meet for the first time, they size each other up without consciously realizing what they are doing—noticing the other's eye and hair coloring, his height and breadth, voice tones, walk characteristics, and a hundred other features. Unguided exposure to music will result in the making of a similar set of observations, and we as teachers should not underestimate how much children can learn about music before they are asked to consciously focus their attention on it. Children exposed to music without comment will automatically appraise it.

Exposing children to music, like exposing them to anything, is a technique that has another function—conditioning. Children who have become accustomed to the sounds of great music will make subconscious and conscious mental associations when they hear those same sounds in the future. Most adults are familiar with the strong preference they seem to have for what they knew in childhood. The person who was brought up on a prairie views the familiar landscape with nostalgia when he is an adult. By the same token, the adult who has been exposed to the music of the masters when he was a child will appreciate it and to some degree enjoy it when he is grown.

Teachers have often been pleasantly surprised at the effects of good music on children. They "key in" quickly and exhibit a decided change in attitude at the first sounds. Some are calmed by it; some work more efficiently while it plays; others will show an overt interest in it. Indeed, they are so sensitive to music, teachers must remember that, if the music they play for them moves at a lively tempo, the children might be inclined to move with it and might become restless and active. Good choices for exposure to music would be the andante, lento, largo, or other slow movement of a symphony or sonata, a barcarolle, a lullaby, a tone poem, music about the sea, clouds, night, a pastoral scene, etc.

A teacher can find many opportune moments to play recordings of music in school—during drawing or painting sessions, as a background for quiet work periods like studying spelling, working on arithmetic, reading silently, practicing writing, etc. At recess time when children must stay indoors, after school when waiting quietly for buses, during lunch time— these are other moments when music can be played. They should be relatively quiet times, and there should not be excessive noise, talking, or distraction in the room. The volume of sound should be at a level which can be heard without being overly intruding.

Giving Children Experiences with Music

After people have had the experience of doing something, they become more interested in it. The person who has tried to paint a picture with oils on canvas comes to see the oil paintings of other people with a visual acuity not present before he made attempts at painting. The person who has experienced a feeling like disappointment or fear will appreciate the sad look of the disappointed person or the nervous look of the fearful. So it is that when people have experienced music, they are more interested in it.

It would not be practical to expect everyone to get experience in writing music in order to heighten their awareness and appreciation of what composers go through when they compose, but it is practical to expect children to have experiences with many of the various aspects of music making. When they sing, they will experience the ups and downs of pitches in melody, the contrasts in rhythms, tempos, dynamics, etc. When they respond to music by dancing, marching, and other movement, they will be feeling rhythms.

The school classroom should be the laboratory in which children experience singing, dramatization of songs, performing basic rhythms, playing instruments, etc., and where, from such experiences, they may arrive at a fuller appreciation of the music they hear.

Training Children in Listening to Music

Two people are together at the same concert. One is a trained musician; the other is an avid music lover who has never formally studied music. Both are enjoying the concert, but the latter suspects that the musician is getting more out of it than he. Is this true? Does the musician know more about the music than the untrained person, and, by knowing more, enjoy it more fully?

To answer the question, imagine this situation. You own a painting which you bought for one reason only—you liked it. Then you were like the untrained music lover. In time, you learned facts about the artist's life and personality, and, thereafter when you viewed your picture, you saw in it colors and brush strokes and other features that seemed to reflect the artist's character. At another time, you learned about the scene the painting portrayed, and from that moment, your eyes read even more meaning into the picture. With every added bit of information, you became more like the trained musician at the concert.

Knowledge that can lead to an increase in appreciation is acquired by people bit by bit. When we train children to listen to music, we should have them notice its components one at a time.

Chief among the components are musical instruments—the media of music. The chapter about instruments in this book gives lesson ideas for teaching children to recognize orchestral instruments by the way they produce sound. The peculiar tone qualities of the various instruments give music its color, and several different instruments playing at the same time can blend well in the same way that several colors in a painting can look well. Children can be trained to hear the distinguishing sounds of each instrument in much the same way as they can be trained to pick out colors in a picture.

Another of the components of music which we can have children notice is the form it takes. Children should be able to recognize a melody when they hear it again or when it returns in a variation. They should be able to find the plan behind the music, to discover how a composition is organized and built up.

Young children can learn to recognize the unique stamp of his own personality which every composer puts upon his music. The methods a composer has of describing a scene with sound, of eliciting moods and feelings in people—these are components which can be studied.

Children of any age can be trained to appreciate music. In fact the same composition can be presented to a sixth grade class as is presented to a first, though of course the listening objectives of each group would be different. For instance, the younger children would only be exposed to a small amount for a short period of time. They might be asked simply to describe the mood of the music or to hear one or two clearcut theme repetitions or identify a predominant instrument. The older children, on the other hand, might be expected to learn about the life of the composer and to relate how he lived to his style of composing. They might be asked to listen for specific themes and be able to describe the overall form, or to explain how instruments were used to help listeners visualize a picture, get a feeling, or feel a mood.

Children who have discovered reasons for why something is so will find it relatively easy to remember what they have learned. To help them remember the four methods of producing musical sound with instruments, the chapter which follows suggests that they consider how these instruments probably originated. To help them remember that composers use repetition of themes to give form to their works, children can be asked to see repetition as a kind of going home, a return to the familiar. Students who have been led to find associations such as these will be more likely to retain what they have learned.

After you have presented the appreciation lessons in this book, look for other compositions to continue training your children in what to listen for. After they have studied a fugue, for example, expose them to another and ask them to apply what they have learned about the first fugue to the new one. The lessons in this book should serve as a springboard for further study of musical compositions.

Chapter 5

YOU CAN TEACH RECOGNITION

OF INSTRUMENTS

One of the chief uses to which man has put his capable brain is to inventing things which extend what he can do with his limited body. Tools like knives, hammers, buckets, and spoons help him do work more easily than he could with teeth, hands, and fingers. The radio and telephone enable his weak ears to hear sounds made miles away. Automobiles, boats, and airplanes transport him more rapidly than could his feet and legs. And musical instruments extend the type of sounds he can make only feebly with his voice, hands, feet and other body parts.

It seems likely that making and playing musical instruments started accidentally and casually, probably in a spirit of play. Surely it was by accident that some ancient man started to fool around with tapping two sticks together. He must have noticed with pleasure that the sounds reminded him of the clapping sounds he could make with his hands and the thumping sounds he could make with his feet. And he must have been pleased that it was an easy job to produce sounds by these artificial means and that the sounds were louder and faster than he could make with his body. He may have found utilitarian value in them when he made loud noises to scare unwanted animals or to signal people some distance away.

At first musical instruments were probably experimented with and played with like toys. The next step was probably to find practical uses, as when man realized that instruments might be used for communications and other services. Their final and present use is to make pleasing sounds which imitate life. Children can easily see that musical instruments copy sounds they know. The violin can hum and whir like a bee or a top, a violin and cello can sound like people conversing, a bassoon can growl like a beast, a wood block can clip-clip like a horse or tick like a clock.

Teaching Recognition of Instruments with This Book

The groups of lessons that follow will teach the recognition of the four prime methods of making sound which are used in today's symphony orchestra. The first lessons will discuss how the group of instruments probably originated and how they might have extended the sounds people made with their bodies. Succeeding lessons will teach children to recognize the sounds of the various instruments from recordings.

In this book the recordings suggested have been chosen because the instrument to be illustrated can be heard clearly either in the melody, or, if it is a background instrument like the harp, as the chief accompaniment. When we ask children to identify instruments from recordings, it is important to keep in mind difficulties that might arise. For instance, the sound of an instrument played by itself gives us one impression, played with other instruments accompanying gives another effect, played in accompaniment of other instruments gives a still different effect. When several of the same instruments combine to play together, the sound is changed, and when two different instruments play the same notes, it can be difficult even for a trained musician to identify them.

The recording should be brief. Ideally, the instrument to be identified does not play all the time, and students must listen carefully and "work" to locate the places where the instrument plays.

The "First Lessons" suggest words you may use in teaching and are most suitable for younger children, although they can be used with older children as well. Motivations, review of material previously learned, etc., are not always given, and you should use your judgment about adding these to your presentations.

The succeeding lessons in recognizing instruments from hearing them on records can be as numerous as you want, depending on how much study your particular class needs, how well you want them to know sounds of instruments, etc. A good procedure is to tell the children what instrument they are to listen for and, if possible, show them a picture of it. If the instrument is featured on the entire recording, tell them to listen quietly so that they may become familiar with its tone, how high and low it can play, the various techniques by which it is played (strings can be plucked or bowed; drums can be beat or rolled, etc.), how different it sounds played fast and slow, loud and soft, and so on. If the instrument is heard only occasionally, ask the children to raise their hands when they first hear it, and lower them when the sound is gone. If the instrument is not familiar (oboe, celesta, etc.), help the children get started by raising your hand with them the first time the instrument is heard. Do not help them with familiar instruments.

Records

To indicate the sources of records, letters and Roman numerals appear in parentheses after each title. (R) indicates that the record is in an RCA Victor "Rhythmic Activities" album, (L) that it is in a "Listening Activities" album. (I, II, III, etc.) refer to grade or album numbers.

THE INSTRUMENTS

Percussion Instruments

Preparation for First Lesson

Have on hand a pair of rhythm sticks or two rulers or two sticks of wood about a foot long. Other rhythm band instruments can be used to supplement the lesson but are not required. Try to have pictures of percussion instruments available.

First Lesson

_____

Long ago, there were no trumpets, no flutes, no drums, no musical instruments at all. When people wanted to make musical sounds, they used their bodies. Can you think of ways to make sounds with different parts of your body?

_____

(The children may show various ways of making sound. Voices can sing, hum, moan, bark; with their mouths they can blow, sigh, click tongues, whistle; their hands can clap, slap thighs, beat chests; fingers can snap; feet can stamp, tap, etc.)

_____

One day many thousands of years ago, a man was walking in the woods, and as he walked, he was tapping together two sticks of wood that he had found on the ground. (Tap the sticks you have to demonstrate this.) At first, he probably thought very little about the sound he was making, but when he finally noticed it, maybe it began to bore and annoy him. Then he probably started experimenting to find different ways of tapping his sticks. Can any of you think of a different way to tap these sticks? Raise your hand if you would like to show us. (Let children take turns. They will think of tapping fast and slow, loud and soft, even and uneven, etc.)

This man of long ago probably had such fun making sounds with sticks that he looked around and found others of different sizes and shapes. Perhaps some were thick and some thin, some hollow inside, but what he noticed as he tapped these different sticks was the difference in their sounds. (Demonstrate this if you have wood blocks, castanets, or other pieces of wood on hand.)

We can hear changes in sound when we tap our bodies in different places. For instance, open your hand, and, when I give the signal, lightly slap your chest four times. . . . Now slap the back of your other hand four times. . . . Slap the inside of your hands. . . . Slap your thigh four times. . . .

Which part of your body made the loudest sound? . . . Which made the highest sounds? . . . Which area sounded hollow inside? . . .

Just as some parts of our body make louder sounds than others when we hit them, so do some pieces of wood sound louder than others. Sometimes the sounds made by hitting hollow logs travel long distances. Can you think how men might have used loud sounds long ago? (Warnings, information, and various messages could be sent to people far away.) Before telephones and radios were invented, people used a musical instrument, the drum, to send messages.

It can be fun to make experiments with an instrument like the drum, to try out different ways of making it sound. With a drum, we can make bigger sounds than we can with our hands and feet, and if you had no telephone, it might be helpful if you had a drum to send messages. But nowadays, people usually play a drum to make music. Drum beats sound like people's feet when they are walking, and they are so loud that when people hear them, they want to dance or march or walk or try to keep up with them.

Today, people use instruments like the drum to make music which will give them pleasure. There are other musical instruments in an orchestra which also are played by hitting or tapping, and these are called the percussion instruments. Can you name some of the percussion instruments which might be found in an orchestra?

(If the children have had experience playing rhythm band instruments, they should name the ones they know: sticks—or rhythm sticks, bells, castanets, claves, cymbals, drums, jingle bells, jingle sticks, maracas, sand blocks, tambourines, triangles, wood blocks, xylophone, etc. An orchestra has many of these, plus: bass drum, celesta, chimes, glockenspiel or bell-lyra, gong, marimba, snare drum, tympani or kettle drums, etc. Show pictures of percussion instruments if available.)

Preparation for Lessons in Recognizing Percussion Instruments

The following record albums have music which demonstrates the sounds of the various percussion instruments: RCA Victor "Rhythmic Activities" (R), Volumes II, III, IV, V, and VI, and RCA Victor "Listening Activities" (L), Volumes I, II and VI. If possible, have pictures of percussion instruments on hand.

Lessons in Recognizing Percussion Instruments

Suggestions for presenting lessons in recognizing instruments appear near the beginning of this chapter.

BELLS: 1. Planquette: "Legend on the Bells" (L I) Bells play the melody throughout this very short composition. 2. Kjerulf: "Elfenspiel" (R III) Bells are heard at the beginning; they play a few chords at the end. 3. Ghys: "Amaryllis" (R IV) In this very short selection bells play the melody the first time through. Strings repeat.

CASTANETS: 1. Saint-Saens: "Tarantelle" (R II) It will be easy for children to hear the castanets in this short selection. 2. Bizet: "Spanish Serenade" (R VI) Castanets play continuously in this relatively long piece of music. If children tire of listening, lower the volume and stop the record.

CELESTA: Poldini: "Waltzing Doll" (L II) The celesta is a small keyboard instrument with hammers inside the mechanism which strike metal bars. It plays the melody in this short selection.

DRUMS

(1) BASS DRUM: Pinto: "March, Little Soldier" (L I) It requires careful listening to hear the bass drum when it comes in at the end with: Boom! (rest) Boom! (rest) Boom boom boom! (rest).

(2) SNARE DRUM: 1. Bizet: "Toreador Song" (R IV) For most of the record, the snare drum plays an even accompaniment. Ask the children to raise their hands only when they hear the drum roll. 2. Bizet: "Street Boys' Parade" (R IV) In this recording we hear the snare drum tap and roll.

(3) TYMPANI: Gluck: "March" ("Iphigenia in Aulis") (R V) This is slow, solemn music. The first theme is played and repeated. Then the trumpet sounds a second theme, and the tympani rolls. Ask the children to identify it when it plays.

TAMBOURINE: 1. Brahms: "Hungarian Dance" (L VI) The tambourine is an instrument used to accompany gypsy dancers. Ask the children to identify the two techniques of playing it after they have listened to the record. (Tapping and shaking) 2. Heller: "Tarantelle" (R III) The tambourine is tapped and shaken throughout this very short piece.

TRIANGLE, CYMBALS: Verdi: "Dance of the Moorish Slaves" (R III) Play the record at least twice. As they listen the first time, ask the children to raise their hands every time they hear the triangle. The second time, ask them to raise their hands when they hear cymbals. Ask them if they can identify any other percussion instruments.

WOOD BLOCK: Kullak: "The Clock" (R III) Two different wood block sounds are heard—one for "tick," the other for "tock." The children will easily recognize the wood block in the three passages where it is played.

XYLOPHONE: 1. Sinding: "March Grotesque" (R V) The xylophone does not come in at the beginning of this music. It is suddenly heard in two quick passages, and, after an interlude, twice again. Strings play pizzicato, and the flute plays a quick scale passage to end the piece. 2. Gardner: "From the Canebrake" (R VI) The xylophone is heard at the beginning of the record. Toward the end it plays a melody and a bit of accompaniment.

Woodwind Instruments

Preparation for First Lesson

Have on hand one or more soda-type bottles and a container of water. Try to have pictures of woodwind instruments (flutes, clarinets, etc.) available.

First Lesson

———————————

One day, long ago, a man was walking in a field with a marsh where wide grasses called reeds are grown. He picked a blade of this grass and aimlessly started to experiment with it. One thing he discovered was that he could hold it stretched firmly, pressed between the sides of his thumbs, and that when he blew across it into the small spaces between his thumbs and the grass, he could make a sharp sound. The tighter he held the blade of grass, the higher the sound he made when he blew. There was such a tiny space for the air to go, he felt his thumbs tingle as the piece of reed vibrated. On that day, this man discovered a different way to make sound.

You can make sounds like this using a wide blade of grass or a piece of paper. (Demonstrating this need not be a part of the lesson, unless it has been practiced beforehand. Suggest to the children that they try this method of producing sound on their own.)

The stems of reed grass are hollow, like tubes. Perhaps on another day long ago, another man was playing with the hollow stem of a reed, and perhaps by accident, he covered the bottom end and blew across the top to make a sound. Perhaps his friends tried it too, but when they picked their reeds, some were long and others were short, and they all sounded different. Do you know how the long ones sounded? (Low) And the short ones? (High)

This soda bottle is shaped like a reed stem, except that it is larger. The empty bottle and an empty reed stem both have something inside them. Do you know what it is? (Air) I will blow across the top of the empty bottle the way the men of long ago blew across the tops of reeds. (Demonstrate.

Press the lip of the bottle against your chin and direct air downward by extending your upper lip out over the top.) Can you tell what happens when air is blown and forced quickly into the bottle? (If the children cannot explain, demonstrate again. The air forced into the bottle will be heard vibrating against the sides.)

To make higher sounds on their reeds, the men who blew them cut them short. But we cannot cut a glass bottle to shorten it. Can you think of something we could do to take away or replace some of the air in a bottle? (We could add water which would replace a like amount of air.) By adding water, there will be less air in the bottle and the sound will be different. (Add water to the bottle and blow across the top.) Can you describe the difference between the sound now and the sound when the bottle was empty? (The pitch would be higher.)

Every time we add water to the bottle, there will be less air, and the sound made when we blow will be higher. (Demonstrate again, or, if there is more than one bottle, you may put varying amounts of water in each and invite different children to blow them. They may be tuned to scale pitches.)

Of course, air vibrating in glass bottles sounds quite faint and a little spooky. Bottles of water would not make good musical instruments. But air vibrating in a tube of wood makes a pleasant and stronger sound, and instruments which are made of wood and are blown to make sound are called woodwinds.

Most woodwind instruments are wooden pipes with holes in them. In the beginning they were all made of wood, but today some of them are made of metal coated with silver. Can you name some of the silver-plated woodwind instruments? (Flutes, piccolos, and sometimes clarinets are silver-plated.)

(If possible, show a picture of a flute or piccolo.) In a flute or piccolo, both ends of the pipe are blocked. The player holds his instrument out to the side and blows across the mouthpiece opening the way we blew across the open bottle top. What does a flute player do when he wants to change to higher or lower notes? (He covers or uncovers holes in the instrument.) Yes, after the player blows air into the mouthpiece, it goes down the instrument until it finds a place to get out. If it must go a long distance to get to an opening, how will it sound? (Low) If it goes a short distance? (High)

Most of the other instruments in the woodwind family are made of wood, and both ends of the pipe are open. The end of the pipe with the mouthpiece (where the player blows) has a smaller opening. There is a little piece of wood called a reed which has been shaved thin and which is clamped against the mouthpiece so that there is only a small space by which the air can pass. The little reed is thin like the blade of reed grass which the early man held with his thumbs and blew against to make sound. Can you name any woodwind instruments which have a reed clamped to the mouthpiece? (Clarinet, bass clarinet, oboe, English horn, saxophone, bassoon, and contra bassoon are the most familiar. The children should be able to name the clarinet and possibly a few others.)

(If available, show pictures of this type of instrument.) To play an instrument like the clarinet, the player must first set the reed in motion by blowing air into the tiny space between the reed and the mouthpiece. The vibrating air then travels down the instrument until it comes to an opening where it can get out.

There are other woodwind-type instruments that are not played in an orchestra but that are sometimes played alone or by classes of children or other small groups of people. Can you think of any like the flute or any that are similar to a clarinet without a reed and perhaps made of a different material? (The children might name tonette, flutophone, recorder, fife, ocarina, sweet potato, etc.)

Preparation for Lessons in Recognizing Woodwind Instruments

The following albums have records which demonstrate the sounds of the various woodwind instruments: RCA Victor "Rhythmic Activities" (R), Volumes II, IV, and V, and RCA "Listening Activities" (L), Volumes II, III, IV, and VI. If possible have pictures of woodwind instruments on hand.

Lessons in Recognizing Woodwind Instruments

Suggestions on presenting lessons in recognizing instruments appeared early in this chapter.

PICCOLO: 1. Pierne: "Entrance of the Little Fauns" (L IV) Sometimes one and sometimes three piccolos can be heard piping. 2. Rebikoff: "Dance of the Chinese Dolls" (L IV) The piccolo plays solos at the beginning, in the middle, and at the end of this oriental-sounding music.

FLUTE: 1. Brahms: "Waltz No. 2" (R II) The flute plays the melody three times in this famous waltz—at the beginning, in the middle, and at the end. 2. Korngold: "Masquerade" (R V) From time to time, the flute plays the melody in this composition. It can also be heard in the background. The children should be able to identify its tones in about a half dozen places.

OBOE: 1. Schubert: "Waltz, Op. 33, No. 2" (R IV) The oboe plays the melody throughout. 2. Schubert: "Waltz, Op. 33, No. 7" (R IV) The children should be able to identify the oboe when it plays. 3. Delibes: "Passepied" (R IV) The oboe is heard playing the melody at the beginning and when the theme is repeated. It is heard twice again—once after the middle section and once toward the end.

CLARINET: 1. Thomas: "Andantino" (L II) The clarinet plays throughout this short composition. 2. Schubert: "Scherzo" (L VI) Strings and woodwinds begin this music. Then the clarinet is heard, playing in a high register. It can be heard clearly twice again, but everyone must listen carefully so as not to miss it.

BASSOON: MacDowell: "Villian" (L III) In this short composition a clarinet and a bassoon in a low register "tiptoe" about.

Stringed Instruments

Preparation for First Lesson

Have available a book, a ruler, and one or more rubber bands. Try also to have pictures of stringed instruments on hand.

First Lesson

One day, long ago, a man was hunting for animals with a bow and arrows. He pulled his bowstring back and released it suddenly. He noticed the sound, and it pleased and fascinated him. He probably wasn't very busy that day, so he spent a lot of time pulling the bowstring and listening to the sound it made.

We can make sound in a similar way, using a rubber band. We will stretch it across a book and raise it with a ruler. (Make the preparation as you talk.) If someone pulls the band and lets it go suddenly, the way the hunter let his bowstring go, we should hear a faint musical sound. (A child may demonstrate.)

That hunter of long ago was probably so pleased with the sound his bowstring was making, we think he may have called his friends to come over with their bows. Then the men took turns plucking their bowstrings and listening to the sounds they made. They soon noticed that, although the bows and strings looked alike, each one made a different sound. Can you guess why there was a difference in the sounds of each string? (Some bows must have been strung more tightly than others.) How would a very tight string sound when let go? (It would sound higher than the looser ones.)

When people play a tune on an instrument, they must make some notes high and others low. Can you think how we could change the pitch of the rubber band on the book? (By pulling the ruler up, away from the book, the rubber band will be tighter.) Let's try what you have suggested. (A child may demonstrate.)

Some of the hunters of long ago were young children, and their bows were shorter than those of the older men. Can you guess how the bowstrings of the smaller bows must have sounded? (Higher than the larger ones) We have discovered two ways of making strings sound higher—by tightening them or by shortening them. Can you think how we could shorten the rubber band or shorten the length of the part we are plucking? (One way would be to move the ruler in or out from the edge of the book to change the length of band being plucked.) Let's try plucking the rubber band with the ruler in one position, then move it to another to see if we can change the sound. (Let the children help demonstrate.)

Musical instruments that make sound by means of vibrating strings are called stringed instruments. Can you think of a small stringed instrument that makes high-pitched sound? (The violin is the highest-pitched stringed instrument in an orchestra. If someone names the "fiddle," tell him that this is a nickname for the violin. Other stringed instruments that produce high sounds are: guitar, banjo, ukelele, and mandolin. Harp, Autoharp, and piano make both high and low sounds.) Can you think of larger stringed instruments that are shaped like the violin but make deeper sounds? (Viola, 'cello, and double bass)

Stringed instruments like the violin and guitar are made with strings stretched across an empty box with at least one hole in it. (If possible, show a picture of a stringed instrument.) Can you guess why such instruments are made with a hollow "box" under the strings? (To make the sound stronger) A string vibrating by itself is weak sounding. With a box under the strings, the sound is both stronger and richer. After the strings start to vibrate, the wood of the box starts to vibrate with them at the same pitch.

Some stringed instruments are plucked or strummed with the fingers, but others are played with a special stick called a bow. This is a long, slender stick which has strands of white hair from horse tails stretched tightly from one end to the other. The hair is rubbed with resin, a gritty substance that scrapes at the strings and helps them to vibrate when the bow is pulled across them. Can you name the stringed instruments which are usually played with a bow? (Violin, viola, 'cello, and bass)

While a violinist is playing, he must shorten the strings of his instrument when he wants to make a higher sound. Do you know how he does this? (He presses the string against the piece of wood under it with one of the fingers of his left hand.) When a violinist must play several notes very fast, he must move the fingers of his left hand very quickly as he presses the strings. At the same time he moves the bow in his right hand swiftly back and forth across the strings.

The piano is a stringed instrument, but we do not usually see the strings of a piano. Do you know how a piano works? (Many young children have observed and a few have figured out that when a piano key is pressed, something inside the piano hits a string to produce sound.) There is at least one string inside the piano for every black or white key outside. These strings are of different lengths with the longest to the left and the shortest to the right.

Which side of the piano will sound lowest? (The left) The piano strings are stretched tight over a huge piece of wood. Why is the wood there? (The sound from the strings is made stronger and more beautiful because the wood vibrates too.)

The harp is a stringed instrument, but its strings are not played with a bow, and it does not have a keyboard like a piano. Do you know how the harp is played? (The strings are plucked by the fingers.)

Preparation for Lessons in Recognizing Stringed Instruments

The following record albums have music which demonstrates the sounds of the stringed instruments of the orchestra: RCA Victor "Rhythmic Activities" (R), Volumes I, III, and VI, and RCA Victor "Listening Activities" (L), Volumes I, II, III, IV, V and VI. If possible, have pictures of stringed instruments on hand.

Lessons in Recognizing Stringed Instruments

Suggestions for presenting lessons in recognizing instruments were offered early in this chapter.

VIOLIN: The majority of compositions for orchestra use violins, and this is a very easy instrument to recognize by sound. Here are a few suggestions for listening: 1. Popper: "Gavotte" (L I) This is a very short violin solo which demonstrates the tone quality of the instrument in both upper and lower registers. 2. Herbert: "Badinage" (L I) This is a short selection in which both pizzicato and bowed playing are heard. In pizzicato the strings are plucked by the fingers without the bow. 3. Schubert: "The Bee" (L III) In this short composition the violin plays very fast, imitating a buzzing bee.

VIOLA: 1. Berlioz: "March of the Pilgrims" ("Harold in Italy") (R VI) The music starts with a string ensemble playing the first theme. This is repeated, after which the cellos play another melody. Then the violas have a solo passage. Violins play pizzicato and while the cellos play a lower part, the violas play the melody. The strings repeat the first theme and play ensemble to the end. (You may have to help the children identify the viola passages.)

CELLO: 1. Rubinstein: "Melody in F" (L II) The cello plays the melody, first in the low register, then in the high. 2. Jarnefelt: "Berceuse" (L II) The violin plays the melody first, then the cello. Violins play again, the cello plays again, and so forth. The children will have to listen carefully to identify the cello.

BASS: 1. Reinhold: "Dwarfs" (R I) The bass plays a solo, and it plucks an accompaniment. Ask the children to find the places where it plays the solo. 2. MacDowell: "Of a Tailor and a Bear" (L II) In this descriptive music, the bass imitates the growls of a bear.

HARP: 1. Weber: "Song of the Shepherdess" (R III) The harp begins and ends this short composition. 2. Ilinsky: "Berceuse" (R III) The harp accompanies most of this music.

PIANO: Most children are familiar with the sounds of the piano, but they may not be aware of the versatility of the instrument or of its ability to give impressions and do imitations. For sheer enjoyment, have them listen to: 1. Goosens: "The Hurdy-Gurdy Man" (L II) The piano imitates the sounds of the hand organ. 2. Chopin: " 'Butterfly' Etude" (L V) Sound is blurred when the pianist's fingers go fast over the keys. Listeners get an impression of whirring wings. 3. Liszt: "Dance of the Gnomes" (L VI) In this music the pianist plays fast and delicately. Staccato, a quick touching of the piano keys, is used to help the listener picture gnomes lightly tiptoeing.

Brass Instruments

Preparation for First Lesson

If possible, have on hand the horn of an animal. Try to have pictures of brass instruments available.

First Lesson

Have you ever looked at the horn of an animal? Did you know that some are hollow or empty inside? (If you have a horn, show the children.) All horns have a pointed end and a wide end.

There must have been a man long ago who noticed how horns were shaped and who decided to try an experiment. Carefully he cut a little piece off the small pointed end of a horn. Then he blew into it and found he could make a sound.

For a long time, people used animal horns for instruments. After metal was discovered, they started making metal horns. These were thin metal tubes with a small end for blowing and a wide bell-shaped end like the broad end of an animal horn out of which came the sound. The person who played one of these instruments would press his lips together tightly so that only a small amount of air could get through. The air he blew into the small end of the horn would travel down the tube and out the bell end. These horns could be heard a long distance away.

Some of the first horns were so long that the bell end rested on the floor or ground. These instruments could only play a few notes, so they could not play many tunes. It has always been easy to play the low notes on a horn. To get higher notes, the player must press his lips together tightly and blow harder.

One day, someone decided that horns were too long. Can you guess what they decided to do? (Curve or bend the tubing) Ever since, the tubing of horns has been curved. If a French horn were stretched out, it would be 16 feet long, but with the tube curled and twisted, a person can easily hold it in his lap.

Do you know what particular metal horns are made from? (Brass) The brass instruments of the orchestra have bell shapes at the end of the tubing. Can you name the instruments in the brass family? (In an orchestra there are the trumpet or cornet, French horn, trombone, and tuba. In a band there might also be bugles, mellophones, baritone horns, alto horns, sousaphones, etc. Show the children pictures of brass instruments if available.)

At one time brass instruments could play only a few notes. Now they can play every note of the scale. Do you know how this is done on the trumpet, French horn, and tuba? (The players press buttons which depress valves.) On an instrument like a trumpet, the player must press and hold a valve when he wants to play a different note. The trumpet has three valves, and each valve is connected to an extra piece of tube. (This can be seen in a picture.) One tube is short, another medium-sized, and the third fairly long. When a valve is pressed down while the player is blowing, the air will be forced through the extra piece of tube. How would you expect the trumpet to sound when the player held down the valve with the short tube connected to it? (Slightly lower) What valve or valves would a trumpet player press if he wanted to make the lowest note possible? (All three valves)

The trombone is a brass instrument which makes all the notes of the scale in a different way. Do you know how this is done? (A sliding tube is pulled out to lower the pitch.) A trombone has one tube inside another. As the player pushes the outside tube out, the notes he is blowing sound lower and lower. A trombone player must learn to feel distances of just a few inches for each note. (Children can guess from a picture how the slide works.)

Preparation for Lessons in Recognizing Brass Instruments

The following record albums contain music which demonstrates the sounds of the brass instruments: RCA Victor "Rhythmic Activities" (R), Volume IV, and RCA Victor "Listening Activities" (L), Volumes I, IV, and V. If possible, have pictures of brass instruments on hand.

Lessons in Recognizing Brass Instruments

Refer to the beginning of the chapter for suggestions in presenting lessons in recognizing instruments.

TRUMPET: 1. Verdi: "March" ("Aida") (R IV) There should be no mistaking the trumpet when it plays solo passages. 2. Wagner: "Festival March" ("Tannhauser") (L V) This is a relatively long piece of music which starts with two trumpets playing fanfares. As the music progresses, we hear their softer tones in a duet and also accompanying other instruments. From about the middle to the end, trumpets play loud duets and fanfares.

FRENCH HORN: Mendelssohn: "Nocturne" ("Midsummer Night's Dream") (L IV) In this brief excerpt, the French horn plays the solo.

TROMBONE: Bizet: "March—Trumpet and Drum" (L I) It is easy to hear the trumpet playing bugle-call music. Listeners should be able to hear the occasional lower tones of the trombone. At the very end, the trombone plays briefly, but clearly.

The Orchestra

Preparation for the Lesson

Have on hand at least one record in 2/4 or 4/4 time with music which alternates from loud to soft. Any of the following are recommended:
Bizet: "March of the Three Kings" (R IV)
Verdi: "Soldiers' Chorus" (R IV)
Reinhold: "War Song" (R V)
Tchaikovsky: "Humoresque" (L IV)
Try to have pictures of an orchestra and the seating arrangement of an orchestra available.

The Lesson

Do you know how many different ways there are of making sound on the musical instruments of an orchestra? (Four) What do we call the group of instruments that is played by tapping or hitting them? (Percussion instruments) What kind of instruments are made of hollow tubes of wood (or silver-coated metal) and are played by blowing? (Woodwind instruments) What do we call the family of instruments that have tightly stretched strings? (Stringed instruments) What do we call the instruments that are made of metal tubing, are shaped like a bell at the end, and are played by blowing? (Brass instruments)

After all the instruments had been invented, the people of long ago who wrote music were curious to hear how it would sound if instruments from all the families played together. They started writing music in which percussion, woodwind, stringed, and brass instruments all had parts to play. When all these people played together, they had a name. Do you know what such a group is called? (An orchestra. If someone uses the term "band," tell him that bands do not include instruments from the stringed group. An orchestra has all four groups.)

Very large orchestras are usually called symphony orchestras, and they have about 100 players in them. They are placed so that every instrument will sound well with the others and so that every one can be heard. Since the stringed instruments are the softest, there are more strings than there are other instruments. There are about 60 players—the violins, violas, and 'cellos are seated across the front, and the basses stand in a row along the back. (A picture of an orchestra or of the orchestra seating arrangement would show this.) There are about 15 woodwind players—flutes, clarinets, oboes, and bassoons—across the middle. At the back are the strongest instruments—the brass and percussion. There are about 15 people playing trumpet, French horn, trombone, and tuba, and about ten people playing drums, triangles, cymbals, and other percussion instruments.

When a symphony orchestra plays, the instruments usually take turns playing. Since everyone doesn't play all the time, and because there are so many people, there has to be some way to let them know exactly when they should come in. And when they do play, they must stay together and all play at the same rate of speed. To help everyone play at the right time, there is a special person who stands in front of an orchestra while it is playing. Do you know what he is called? (A conductor) An orchestra conductor leads the players, signaling them to start and helping them stay together. If he talked out loud to tell them these things, it would spoil the music. There is another way he signals everyone. Do you know what it is? (He signals the players with his hands and arms.)

Whenever an orchestra conductor moves his arms, music sounds. When he stops, the sounds stop. It is almost as if the orchestra were an instrument which played when the conductor moved his arms.

It would be difficult for us to learn to play an instrument like the violin or the trumpet without a lot of work and practice. But we can all pretend to be orchestra conductors. Before we try it with music, let's practice. Remember, we cannot talk, only move our arms. Hold your arms ahead of you at about shoulder level. Make a slight bend at the elbow. Now let your arms drop down about a foot and make a little bounce when they "hit bottom." After the little bounce, go straight up to where you started. Try it again until you can make your arms move down-up, down-up evenly, doing the little bounce without stopping or changing rhythm.

Now try it with the music on this record. (Play the record.)

As you listened to the music, did you notice that part of it was loud and part of it soft? If you were a real orchestra conductor, you would have to signal everyone when you wanted them to play loud or soft. Remember that you could not talk. How would you signal everyone to play loudly?

(The children may discuss this and individuals may demonstrate.) What would you do if you wanted the orchestra to play softly? (Again, the children discuss it.)

When you hear the record this time, you will have three things to tell the orchestra with your arms as you are conducting. First, you must tell them when to start; second, tell them how fast to play; and third, tell them when to play loud or soft.

Timbre

This lesson is most suitable for children in grades 3 to 6.

Preparation for the Lesson

This lesson must be presented in a room with a piano, preferably a grand piano. If this is not available, an upright is to be preferred to a smaller piano. The children should be positioned as near to the instrument as possible.

Have available another melody instrument that can match a tone with a tone on the piano. A toy xylophone, tonette, or Autoharp will be satisfactory. Before the lesson starts, find a note on the piano that is of the same pitch as one on the other instrument.

The Lesson

Have you ever noticed that when two different instruments play the same note, the note sounds very different on each one? Listen as I play the same note on the piano and on this other instrument. (Demonstrate, playing the note first on one instrument, then on the other a few times.) The difference in sound is called a difference in timbre (pronounced TIMber or TAMber).

Scientists discovered that the reason there is a difference in the timbre of instruments is that a single note is not really one note but several. That is, there is the one note we hear plainly, and there are several other tones which sound faintly. Listen while I strike a note on the piano. Try to hear the faint notes. Keep the room as quiet as possible. (Strike a note at the far left end of the keyboard, using as much force as possible, and keep it depressed for about 15 seconds.) Did you hear more notes than the one which was played? (Children may discuss the question.)

The extra notes which you heard faintly are called overtones because they are over or higher-sounding than the strong note. (Another name for these is partials. Sometimes they are called harmonics.) A note played on a piano will have one set of overtones, while the same note played on, say, a clarinet will have an entirely different set. When we hear a note, then, our ears hear all the overtones as well, and this is how we can tell if the note was played by an oboe or a trumpet or a violin or any other instrument.

It is very difficult to locate the exact overtones of a note without scientific equipment, but we can do an experiment which will prove that overtones exist. To help conduct the experiment, I will need an assistant. (Choose a child to be with you at the piano.)

When a note is sounded, it vibrates, and when it vibrates it can set other things with the same pitch to moving or vibrating. It is like what happens when you want to get a particular apple from a branch of an apple tree. As you shake the branch with the apple you want, other branches with other apples will shake too. As you play a note on the piano and cause it to vibrate, the strings of its overtones will vibrate too, if they are free to do so.

To free a string, we must lift the hammer from it. This can be done by holding down the key. I am going to ask my assistant to press the key which is eight notes above the key I am going to play. Do not play the note, only hold it silently, holding the key and not letting it go. The note being held will probably be an overtone. If it is, you will hear the string sound after I strike the lower note.

(As soon as the child is holding the key, strike your note quickly and hard and let go immediately. The string connected to the key the student is holding should be heard vibrating. If it is not, repeat the experiment with the key eight notes higher.)

Let's continue experimenting with notes to see if we can find any more overtones. This time, my assistant may choose a note, any note, as long as it is above the one I am playing. As he holds it, see if you hear it vibrating. What will you know if you hear it sound? (It is an overtone.) If you do not hear any sound from the string, what will that prove? (It is not an overtone.)

(Continue the experiment for as long as the students are interested. It is a good idea to be systematic, testing every note of the scale, including black notes, until all the strong overtones have been located.)

Chapter 6

YOU CAN TEACH MUSIC LISTENING

Training students in what to listen for in music is like training them in any skill. In the beginning the learners are made conscious of certain of the components of a specific composition. To get practice in using what has been learned, students should be expected to transfer what they have learned about one piece to other music like it. For instance, after completing the lessons about the "Scherzo" by Mendelssohn, they should, under the guidance of the teacher, listen to other scherzos and to other works by the composer Mendelssohn.

The lessons which follow suggest focusing on certain points of study: learning about the composer, identifying instruments, discovering the picture, the feeling, or the mood intended, recognizing themes when they recur or when they are played in variation in forms like the fugue, the rondo, the symphony, or the dance, picturing stage performance from hearing the music which accompanies it, and interpreting music with body motion.

The Composer

All music starts in the mind of a composer. What he writes and how he writes it depend on many factors—his inherited intellectual and musical ability, the influence parents and other people had on him when he was a child, how the climate and topography of his country affected him, the impact of the events of the times in which he lived, his state of health, the degree to which he was financially independent, how well his work was accepted. These factors and more contribute heavily to the final result.

Students should be told about the lives of composers because children, like grown-ups, are curious about how other people live. They can compare their own behavior with that of composers when they were children and, by noting similarities and differences, can learn about themselves. Younger children will be interested to learn of the accomplishments of the child Mozart and to find out, for instance, what toys Handel preferred when he was a child. Older children will understand how factors like poverty, illness, deafness, fame, and the like might contribute to the creation of music. They will find inspiration in the lives of men like Mozart, who was kept poor and unknown by contemporaries who were jealous of his genius, or Beethoven, who suffered mental agony brought on by depression, paranoia, and physical torment from his deafness, or Mendelssohn, who was never spoiled by wealth and popularity. Children can discuss the ability of men of genius to triumph over obstacles. They should be encouraged to read supplementary material about composers' lives.

Instruments

Musical instruments are the media of the composer. The study which was started in Chapter 5 is applied to the listening lessons of this chapter.

Descriptive Music

There are certain compositions in which a composer has tried consciously to depict a scene or tell a story, and, for these compositions, students should be told the titles and as much as possible about the intentions of the composer. However, it should be remembered that music titles are not exact, and we cannot insist that students picture only what the title suggests. On the other hand, it is not wise, as a rule, to ask children to guess a title by listening to the music, for they will often make an assortment of mostly wrong guesses, and there is a good chance they will remember one or more of them.

A name or a title is a convenient means of identifying things. It is easy to name a representational drawing or a photograph, but, when naming a musical composition, identification can never be certain. For example, the first movement of Beethoven's "Moonlight" Sonata with its calm tempo, its quiet, steady passage of chords from one arpeggio to the next, helps the listener to envision a peaceful, moonlight scene; but, one could just as easily imagine a boat gliding on smooth water in broad daylight, or a person lamenting a lost love. Brahms' famous "Lullaby" could as easily remind listeners of moonlight as of someone singing to a child.

A wise procedure in presenting descriptive music is to give students the title, but not insist that it represents the only possible picture to be derived from the sounds in the music. Children should not be discouraged from thinking of alternative pictures. They should decide how well the composer has accomplished the task of helping listeners to picture something specific.

Ask them to name the elements of tempo or rhythms, of tone or volume, of instrumentation, etc., which have combined to remind them of the scene or action named.

Feeling or Mood in Music

Children and grown-ups alike are aware that music can help them feel calm or agitated, happy or sad, fearful or secure. A composer has various means at his disposal for eliciting such feelings.

First, he has tempo or rate of speed. When people are afraid, they might move quickly, furtively, or perhaps in uneven rhythm, and when calm, they would probably move smoothly or with assurance. A composer can write music in tempos and rhythms that will remind people of such feelings. He can use pitch to bring out feelings. By keeping a melody high, people will feel tense, and will want to tense their muscles in accord with the music. Lower tones will help the listener feel relaxed. The composer can use different modes to bring on moods. The major will make the listener feel optimistic, happy, secure, peaceful, etc., while music in the minor mode, with the third and sixth tones of the scale lowered, can make him feel sad, depressed, frightened, or in some way uneasy.

Another device which the composer can use to remind people of feelings is to have particular instruments play. A flute played in the low register, which uses "breathy" tones, might remind them of warmth and comfort. Sharp-toned trumpets can stir people into feeling alert. Martial-sounding drums can remind them of such feelings as dignity and orderliness.

By using different dynamics, varying the loudness of the music, the composer can evoke certain feelings in people. When the music suddenly becomes soft, the audience will become attentive and expectant. A sudden loud chord may startle or disturb everyone.

A composer induces feelings by means of his accompaniment. For instance, full chords which are held onto can help make people feel reverent or noble or in some way elevated. Broken chords or arpeggios can give a feeling of motion and temporariness.

Children should be made aware of the mood-making devices available to composers and should attempt to describe them in words.

Recurrence of Themes

When composers write music, they almost invariably choose to repeat tunes. Repetition is important to life, and we see it when people choose to return to familiar places or when they repeatedly demand their favorite foods. Children will readily "understand" the interest composers have in repeating thematic material.

The order in which themes are repeated gives music its form. In referring to such repetition, it is customary to label themes with letters of the alphabet. By calling the first tune "A," the second "B," the third "C," etc., the form of a composition can be charted.

The simplest form is simple repetition—A A—and is called two-part form. Three-part form would be A B A with a second tune intervening between the two A's. A form in which several tunes intervene between the A's—A B A C A D A, etc.—is called the rondo.

One of the more interesting forms which will be explained in succeeding lessons is the fugue. Here the main theme, the "subject," is repeated in different registers, starting on different notes. The intriguing aspect of this form is that the end of the theme must blend with its beginning in such a way that, throughout the fugue, two, three, four or more voices may be heard simultaneously. Children enjoy this form and like to be challenged to identify the recurring theme each time it enters.

Development of Themes

In music, the term "development" refers to the repetition of material in various ways—with embellishments added, with different accompaniments, using different instruments, perhaps with different harmonies or in different modes. Children can be helped to understand this device if we remind them that a particular person is still the same person, no matter what clothes he is wearing. John is still John, whether he is in a snow suit or a Halloween costume. A tune is still the same tune, whether it is played by a violin or by a tuba.

The first movement of a symphony or a sonata uses this technique of working with material. The first part of the movement, called the exposition, usually presents two themes—one strong and masculine, the other gentle and feminine. The part which follows is called the development, and in this part, tunes are heard in different ways, "dressed up," so to speak. There is usually an increase in tension as the themes are put into their various disguises. At the end of the movement is heard a restatement of the original themes. This is called the recapitulation. Children should be asked to discover the ways in which a composer develops or varies his themes.

Dance Form

Before the symphony and sonata form were developed around 1750, composers chose to pattern much of their large orchestral music after dances of the day. These were grouped in suites and were to be listened to, not danced.

The dance suite viewed as a whole demonstrates the composer's attempt to keep his listeners interested. One device for holding attention was to write all dances in the same or related keys. A second device was to keep them short, usually in two or three divisions (A B or A B A). Another means for keeping people's attention was to vary the tempos and time signatures from dance to dance. For example, a suite might start with a moderately fast allemande in 4/4, proceed to a courante in a quick 3/4, move on to a slow saraband in 3/4, and end with a lively gigue in 12/8. Older children will be especially interested in seeing how composers used variety in tempo to influence people psychologically.

The individual dances of composers like Bach and Handel were interesting and enjoyable by themselves. Among the more popular were the minuet, gavotte, gigue, hornpipe, and bourrée. After they have heard some of this lilting music, children will understand why such dances appealed to people of earlier times and why composers chose to pattern large-scale orchestral music on this relatively simple form.

Music to Accompany Stage Performances

Among the more important compositional works are those written to accompany stage performances. They include music for ballet, dance, opera or music drama, and incidental music performed between scenes or acts of plays.

Children who are to listen to this music should be told the story and what scenery, costumes, characters, and stage action to picture. As they listen, they should try to find sounds in the music which remind them of the traits of the characters, their feelings, the action, etc.

Moving to Music

When people listen to music, they respond to it in various ways—nodding heads, tapping toes, swinging legs. This is especially true when people hear dance music.

Children, too, will unconsciously respond to rhythmical music, and there will be times when you might want to invite them to interpret what they are hearing with larger body motions. For instance, when form is being taught, different groups could move to the different sections; when a composition is predominantly rhythmical, a dance could be created; if the scene the music pictures is known, it could be acted out. However, not all music should be interpreted. If the goal of the listeners is to hear the tone color of instruments or to discover mood, or, if the music is very fast or intricate, such music should only be listened to.

Teaching Music Listening with This Book

The lessons for the first group of compositions which follow present ideas which can best be used with students in the first three primary grades. Presentations for the last group are suited to intermediate grade children of about fourth through sixth grades.

Two or three lessons are suggested, but classroom teachers might stretch these out to any number. There could be several five to ten-minute sessions, starting with periods when the record is played without comment. These might be further supplemented with listening to other music by the same composer or to other compositions with similar titles or in the form that was studied.

The words suggested for the lessons should serve as an impetus for teaching, and motivation, review, and other teaching devices should be used at the discretion of the teacher.

THE LISTENING LESSONS

"Badinerie" from "Suite in B Minor" (Primary)
Johann Sebastian Bach
Germany, 1685–1750

Preparation for the Lessons

The music is in "Adventures in Music," Grade III, Volume 1.

First Lesson

Many years ago there lived in Germany a man named Johann Sebastian Bach. He spent most of his life composing church music, and, for fun, he wrote music for his family to sing and play in the evenings after work. He also wrote dance music for people to listen to. In those days, 250 years ago, people liked dance music so much that composers often wrote such music for people to sit and listen to without dancing.

Today we are going to hear one of those pieces of dance music that was written for listening only. Bach wrote it while he was the director of music for a prince of Germany. The prince liked to entertain his friends by having his orchestra play music written especially for him. His friends were very wealthy people who were accustomed to hearing special entertainments.

Imagine that you are a friend of Bach's prince. You have just finished a delicious dinner, and you are now sitting in a beautifully-decorated room which has fancy fabrics and expensive furniture. The people are wearing splendid clothing, and the ladies are wearing beautiful jewels. The room suddenly becomes quiet and you hear someone announce that the orchestra will play a new composition by the director, Johann Sebastian Bach. It is called "Badinerie" (bah-din-A-ree).

(Play the record.)

As you listened to "Badinerie," did you feel like dancing, or was it easy to sit still? (Children may discuss the question.) The name of the music, "Badinerie," is a very old word which was not so much the name of a dance as it was a word for tumbling and acrobatics. But, whichever was meant, doing stunts or dancing, the music was lively enough to make everyone feel like moving about.

Second Lesson

At our last lesson, we heard a dance-type piece of music written many years ago by a famous German composer. Do you remember his name? (Johann Sebastian Bach) For whom did Bach write the music? (For the prince for whom he worked)

The music which we heard was written and first played at about the time our first president, George Washington, was living. Have you ever seen pictures of Mr. Washington or of people of those times? Can you tell us how they were dressed? (Men wore tight pants down to the knee, knee stockings, tight jackets with lace at the wrists and neck, etc. Ladies wore hoop skirts, and everyone wore white powdered wigs on their heads.) You can imagine how difficult it would have been for people dressed like that to dance to the fast music we heard. This is one reason we are sure the "Badinerie" was music to sit and listen to and was not for dancing.

As the people listened, they watched the orchestra play. There was one man who played a particular instrument, and he was the man who played the happy tune which seems to run and hop about. All the other instruments played in the background. As you listen to the record today, see if you recognize the instrument that plays the happy tune and the other instruments that play in the background.

(Play the record.)

What instrument played the happy tune? (Flute) What instruments played in the background? (Violins and strings)

Third Lesson

What was the name of the dance-type music we heard at our last listening lessons? ("Badinerie") Who was the composer? (Johann Sebastian Bach) When we listened last time, we found out that a flute was playing the melody and stringed instruments were playing the accompaniment.

Today we are going to listen to the melody. Near the middle of the whole composition, we should notice a change in the tune. Actually, this will be the beginning of the second tune, because "Badinerie" has two different tunes.

Tunes are like friends. After you have met them once, you see them again. After you have heard the first tune in "Badinerie," you will hear it again. The second tune will also come back like an old friend.

Raise your hand every time you hear a tune begin. Raise your hand at the beginning to show that you are listening to the beginning of the first tune. Put it down, and wait until you hear the very same music start again, when you should raise your hand once more. When the tune ends that time, the second tune will begin. Raise your hand then and once more when it returns.

(Play the record.)

When you discovered the plan of the tunes in "Badinerie," you were discovering the plan behind many other pieces of dance music.

The Music Box (Primary)
Anatol Liadov
Russia, 1855–1914

Preparation for the Lessons

The music is in RCA Victor "Listening Activities," Volume V; Musical Sound Books 78016; Bowmar Orchestral Library #64. Try to have a music box or a picture of a music box available.

First Lesson

A hundred or more years ago, before radios and record players and tape recorders had been invented, people listened in their homes to the tinkling sounds of music boxes. (Show a music box or a picture of one if it is available.)

Some music boxes were small, and some were large, but inside all of them, the mechanism was very similar. There would be a metal disc with projecting points, and there was a spring which had to be wound with a key to make the disc turn. As it slowly turned, the metal points passed over prongs, every one of which made the sound of a different note of the scale. As the projecting points passed the prongs, they picked them and made them sound. Discs could be made with points arranged to play any song or tune the maker wanted.

Of course, large music boxes had big prongs and wide discs, and little boxes had short prongs and small discs. What was the difference in sound between the large and small music boxes? (The large ones made deep, strong sounds; the small ones high, light sounds.)

The music we shall be hearing today is called "The Music Box." You will soon discover that an orchestra is trying to imitate a music box playing. Decide as you listen whether it is supposed to be a large box or a small one. Also, listen for what instruments are used to imitate the music box. I will play just enough of the record for you to be able to tell.

(Play the record a minute, lower the volume and stop.)

Was it a large or a small music box? (Small) What instruments were used to imitate the sounds of a real music box? (Everyone will be able to name the flute and bells. Older children should recognize also the piccolo, the harp accompaniment, clarinet and oboe.)

A music box is mechanical, and, like a mechanical toy, once it has been wound up, it will play on and on, repeating its tunes again and again. This music box has more than one tune, and, as we listen to the record this time, I would like you to see how well you can recognize the first tune every time it begins.

The record will begin with a short introduction. When that is over, the first tune will come in. Raise your hands for a moment when you hear it. Then put them down and wait until you hear the same tune start again. Let's see how many times the first tune comes back.

(Play the entire record. The first tune—A—comes in eight times. The pattern is: A A B B A C D—A A B B A C D—A B A.)

Second Lesson

At our last listening lesson, we heard music played by an orchestra that was trying to imitate an old-fashioned instrument. What was it? (A music box) There were many kinds of music boxes, some big and some small. Some were hidden in the bottom of a lady's powder box, and some that were hidden in mugs played when the mug was lifted. But usually, the mechanical part was inside a wooden box with a painted picture or a carving on the outside.

At our last lesson, you discovered the first tune every time it came in. There are other tunes in this music box, and today, we will try to count how many and see how they are arranged.

On the chalk board we will make a picture of the arrangement of tunes, showing the order in which they are played. (If the children are in third grade or older, one or more of them may be at the board. Otherwise, you, the teacher, should write the pattern.) We will call the first tune by the first letter of the alphabet—A—and the second tune by letter B. If another tune comes in, we will call it C. You may help me (or "us," if there are children at the board) know when to write a letter by raising your hands when you hear a tune begin. Remember to wait until the introduction is over.

(Play the record. After the introduction, the person at the board will write: A (repeat of A) B (repeat of B) (repeat of A) C and D. The pattern is repeated: A (A) B (B) (A) C D. At the end is heard A B A.)

Whenever a composer writes music, he has a plan for his tunes, and you have discovered the plan for "The Music Box." He also wants you, his listeners, to get a picture of whatever the music is about. What happened at the end of this music which would remind you of what would happen if a real music box was playing? (The music slowed down, as if the music box needed to be wound up again.)

Golliwogg's Cakewalk (Primary)

Claude Debussy
France, 1862–1918

Preparation for the Lessons

The music is in RCA Victor "Listening Activities," Volume II; Musical Sound Books 78037; Bowmar Orchestral Library #63.

First Lesson

Many years ago in France, the composer, Claude Debussy (deb-oo-SEE) wrote a group of piano pieces for his five-year-old daughter. He called it "The Children's Corner Suite," and ever since he wrote it, the music has been enjoyed by grown-ups and children alike throughout the world. One of the pieces describes the fall of snow; another is a song for a doll; another is about a toy elephant being sung to sleep; and another imitates the music a shepherd boy plays while watching his sheep.

The piece we are going to hear from "The Children's Corner Suite" is called "Golliwogg's Cakewalk." Does anyone know what a golliwogg is? (If anyone knows, he may answer.) A golliwogg is a rag doll which is dressed like a clown in baggy clothes and which has a lot of hair sticking straight out from its head.

You can almost guess from the name what a "cakewalk" must be—a walk around a cake! This is what it was many years ago when people would make up a dance around a table with a delicious-looking freshly-baked cake on it. Whoever made up the best dance received a prize. Can you guess what it was? . . . Yes, the cake was the prize! Some years later there was a dance called the cakewalk which was performed on the stage during minstrel shows.

As you listen to "Golliwogg's Cakewalk," picture a loose-jointed rag doll with floppy hair dancing around a table with a big cake on it. The doll is grinning, and it holds its head high. As it dances, it keeps its eyes on that tempting cake.

Right in the middle of the piece, the music slows. Can you guess why? (Perhaps the golliwogg tires of dancing.) Probably the golliwogg needs a rest. He keeps on dancing but not as fast as before. In fact, sometimes the music stops entirely.

After the slow part, the fast cakewalk music starts again, and away goes the golliwogg, doing his funny, happy dance. When you hear the cakewalk music start again, raise your hands for a moment. Be careful to wait until the slow part is over before you signal that you hear the fast part starting up again.

(Play the record.)

Second Lesson

At our last listening lesson, we heard music which described a funny doll doing a dance. Do you remember the name of it? ("Golliwogg's Cakewalk") What is a golliwogg? (A rag doll with floppy hair and loose joints which is dressed in baggy clothing.) What is a cakewalk? (Originally it was a dance done around a table with a cake on it.)

Today while the music plays, you may pretend to be golliwoggs doing a cakewalk dance. There will be two groups, and each group will have a turn to make up a dance. (Divide the class into groups.)

Group One may start, and Group Two may watch and clap lightly in time with the music. Pretend there is a cake on a table and you are dancing around it. When you hear the slow part in the music, Group Two will stop clapping, and everyone will move their feet to dance in place. When the fast part returns, Group One will stand back and clap lightly while Group Two has a turn to make up a dance.

(Play the record for dancing.)

Entrance of the Little Fauns (Primary)
Gabriel Pierné
France, 1863–1937

Preparation for the Lessons

The music is in RCA Victor "Listening Activities," Volume IV; Musical Sound Books 78015; Bowmar Orchestral Library #54.

First Lesson

Did you ever see a picture of a faun or a satyr? . . . They were make-believe creatures who were supposed to have lived in the forest. The upper parts of their bodies were like men, except that they had short horns and little pointed ears. They had the tails and legs of a goat with hoofs instead of feet.

Today we are going to hear music called "Entrance of the Little Fauns." As the music plays, we are supposed to imagine these little make-believe creatures marching in line through the forest. At the head of the line is their teacher, an old satyr, who is giving them a lesson in playing Panpipes. The Panpipe is a very old instrument made up of hollow wooden pipes of different lengths bound together and played by blowing across the open tops.

As the music starts, you will easily hear the sounds of the hoof-beats of the little fauns as they march through the woods. A trumpet tune helps them keep in step. When you think you hear the Panpipes playing, raise your hands and keep them up all the time you hear them, lowering them when the sound of the pipes stops.

(Play the record.)

Do you know the name of the instrument which played the Panpipe music? (Piccolo) Did you notice how the music ends? (It softens and fades away.) Why do you suppose the music gets softer at the end? (Perhaps the fauns leave the scene or vanish from sight.)

Second Lesson

At our last listening lesson we heard music called "Entrance of the Little Fauns." What were fauns supposed to have looked like? (Half-man and half-goat) What were the fauns doing as they marched along? (Having a lesson in playing Panpipes)

"Entrance of the Little Fauns" is part of a story which is danced on a stage and is called a ballet. In this part of the ballet, the little fauns are in a forest having a lesson from their teacher, an old satyr.

We can pretend that we are in the ballet on the stage. One person may be the "teacher," and the ones who play the part of the fauns may follow him. (Choose one child to be the teacher. A small group may be chosen or the whole class may be the fauns.) The forest has many trees, and the teacher will lead you around them. Listen carefully so that your feet will stay with the music.

(Play the record for the children to move in procession.)

Little Train of the Caipira (Primary)
Heitor Villa-Lobos
Brazil, 1887–1959

Preparation for the Lessons

The music is in "Adventures in Music," Grade III, Volume 1; Bowmar Orchestral Library #64.

First Lesson

Today we are going to hear music called "Little Train of the Caipira" (kī-PEER-a). It describes a little train in Brazil which moves through the countryside picking up the caipira or farm workers and brings them to the big farm where they will work for the day. By listening to the music we should be able to find out what is happening. Instead of someone to tell us with words, there will be an orchestra to make the sounds of the train and of the people.

If you could hear a train without seeing it, what are some of the sounds you might expect to hear? (The engine chugging, wheels clicking along the tracks, whistle blowing, etc.) How would the sounds change if the train had to climb a steep hill? (You would hear it gradually slowing and chugging harder until it got over the hump of the hill, and then it would roll along as before.)

The caipira are happy people, and you will hear their happy tune when you listen to the music. Try to guess what they are doing. Try to guess what happens from the sounds in the music.

(Play the record.)

Could you guess what the caipira were doing as they rode in the train? (Singing a song. The composer has used the melody of a Brazilian folk song.) Could you tell what was happening by listening to the sounds in the music? (The train started to move slowly. As it rushed along the tracks, the caipira sang a song. It slowed down when it climbed a steep hill. When it got to the other side of the hill, it rushed along again as before. The whistle tooted, and, toward the end, you could hear the pistons of the engine moving up and down and sounds of air escaping as the brakes were put on and the train came to a stop.)

Second Lesson

At our last music listening lesson we heard "Little Train of the Caipira." Who were the caipira? (Farm workers in Brazil) Where were they going in the train? (To a big farm to work) What were they doing as they rode along? (Singing a song) Why did the music slow down? (The train must have come to a steep hill.)

In your imagination you were able to "see" the little train and guess what must have been happening even though there was no picture and no one to tell you in words what the train looked like or what was happening. This means that you must have listened carefully.

Today you may make "little trains" and when you hear the music, you may move to it. (Choose one group or several to make "little trains.") The first person in the group will be the engine. You will all move with the music until it starts to slow down. This will be a signal to the "engine" to pull the other "cars" up the hill. Then listen for the music to tell you when to move as you were moving before. Move as quietly as possible so that we can all hear the record. Do not make train sounds, but let the orchestra make them for us.

———————————

(Play the record for the children to move as trains.)

Children's Symphony, 1st and 3rd movements (Primary)

Harl McDonald
USA, 1899–1955

Preparation for the Lessons

The first movement is in "Adventures in Music," Grade III, Volume 2. The third movement is in "Adventures in Music," Grade II.

First Lesson

Many years ago, after musical instruments had been invented, composers started to write music in which all the instruments would play together. Do you know what the whole group of players was called? (An orchestra)

A large orchestra with about 100 players is called a symphony orchestra, and the music we are to hear today is called a symphony. When you listen, you will notice that sometimes all 100 instruments play together, and sometimes you will hear only one. Sometimes 30 violins will play at once, and sometimes you will hear nothing when all the instruments are quiet.

A symphony is a piece of music which is so long it must be divided into four parts. Each part is called a movement and moves at a different rate of speed. The first movement is played medium fast, the second slow, the third gay and dance-like, and the fourth fast and exciting. The composer of a symphony makes these changes in speed so that people will not get tired of listening.

Today we are going to hear the first movement of "Children's Symphony," which was written by the American composer, Harl McDonald, in 1950. There are rules for writing the first movement of a symphony. You already know the rule for speed. How fast must the first movement go? (Medium fast) That is the rule for speed. Another rule is that there must be two tunes—the first strong and the second weak. The first tune must be played twice, and then it must be played a few more times, every time changed in some way. Changing a tune is something like dressing a person in different clothing. It is still the same person whether he is wearing a bathing suit or a clown costume, and a tune is still the same tune whether it is played by a flute or by a trombone.

That is one way to change a tune, to have it played by different instruments. Another way might be to have it played very slowly or to make it sound sad. If extra notes were played, the same tune could sound more fancy.

After the first tune in the first movement of the symphony has been played in different ways, the second tune must come in quietly, sounding sweet and gentle. At the end of the movement, Tune Number One is supposed to come back stronger than ever.

You know the two tunes in the first movement of "Children's Symphony" very well. As you listen to it, try to remember what ways the first tune is changed or "dressed up."

(Play the record.)

What was the first tune? ("London Bridge") What was the second tune? ("Twinkle, Twinkle, Little Star" or "Baa, Baa, Black Sheep") How did the composer change or "dress up" "London Bridge"? (He had different instruments play it; he made it sound sad; he stretched it out with extra notes.)

The second tune came in so quietly and slowly that it was hard to recognize what it was. Which tune played at the end? ("London Bridge") How was it playing? (Loudly, gaily, in march rhythm)

Second Lesson

At our last music listening lesson, we heard the first movement of "Children's Symphony." We found out that there are rules for writing the first movement of a symphony. First, how fast should it go? (Medium fast) How many tunes should it have? (Two) What song tunes did the composer use in "Children's Symphony"? ("London Bridge" and "Twinkle, Twinkle, Little Star") About how many instruments were playing in the symphony orchestra? (About 100)

In a symphony, the instruments take turns playing, and once in a while, they all play together. For instance, the first time we hear "London Bridge," the flutes play it, and the second time, it is played by the violins. Finally, almost everyone in the orchestra is playing as loud as they can! Then the drums play alone, as if to say: "Attention, everybody! The second tune is about to be played!"

Today as you listen to "Children's Symphony," pay particular attention to the second tune, "Twinkle, Twinkle, Little Star." Try to remember which group of instruments—stringed, brass, or woodwind—plays the tune the first time softly and which group repeats the tune, playing it loudly. The drums will play again, as if to say: "Attention, everybody! The first tune is coming back!" Then the first tune will come back to end the first movement with drums drumming and cymbals clashing.

(Play the record.)

What was the first group of instruments that played "Twinkle, Twinkle, Little Star" softly? (Strings—violins first, then 'cellos) Which group repeated it loudly? (The brass group—trombones first, then trumpets)

Third Lesson

At our last two music listening lessons, we heard the first movement of a long piece of music. What was it called? ("Children's Symphony") How many parts or movements are there in a whole symphony? (Four) Why are some of these movements fast and some slow? (So that listeners will not get tired or bored) How fast did the first movement go? (Medium fast) The second movement is always slow, the third is gay and dance-like, and the fourth is very fast.

Today we are going to hear the third movement of "Children's Symphony." As it begins, you will hear an introduction that runs and skips gaily along. Then you will hear a tune which you will recognize easily. Later you will hear a second tune which you will also know. Between the tunes, you will be hearing trumpets play bugle calls.

As you listen to the third movement of "Children's Symphony," try to remember the names of the two song tunes. Listen for the trumpets to play bugle calls, and show by raising your hands that you recognize them. Put your hands down as soon as each bugle call is over.

(Play the record.)

What was the first song tune in the third movement of "Children's Symphony"? ("The Farmer in the Dell") What was the second well-known tune? ("Jingle Bells")

"Polka" from "The Age of Gold" (Primary)
Dmitri Shostakovitch
Russia, 1906–

Preparation for the Lessons

The music is in RCA Victor "Listening Activities," Volume VI; Musical Sound Books 78104.

First Lesson

There are many ways of telling a story. If a teacher wanted to tell his class a story, how might he do it? (He might read it from a book, tell it from memory, etc.) If you were given a piece of paper and a pencil and you were told that you could not speak words or write them, could you still tell a story? (Yes, by drawing pictures) Now, imagine that you have no paper and pencil, no way of making pictures, and you are not allowed to talk. Could you still tell a story? (Yes, by dancing, pantomime, hand signals)

People sometimes tell a story by dancing it on a stage. Such a dance is usually called a ballet. The music we are to hear today is part of a ballet called "The Age of Gold." We will not hear all of the ballet music, only the part called "Polka."

A polka is a fast dance in which the dancers walk forward three steps and on the fourth count, hop. Couples dance around the room with a step, step, step, hop; step, step, step, hop.

The music begins with a short introduction while the dancers get ready on the ballet stage. As they do the polka, they pretend they are serious, but they are really making fun of the people who are trying to bring peace to the world by recommending disarmament in an organization called the League of Nations.

As you listen to "Polka" from "The Age of Gold" ballet, the sounds in the music may remind you of other things, perhaps something mechanical like a robot or a merry-go-round. Imagine whatever you want to, but decide as you are listening how the music makes you feel—happy, sad, serious, amused, frightened, or what.

(Play the record.)

Was that serious music?... Was it sad?... Was it frightening?... Was it funny?... (Most children agree that it was funny.) Did the music remind you of anything? (Encourage the children to tell what they may have imagined—a robot clanking and clattering about, a telephone company, a clock factory with machinery breaking down! It is easy to imagine a humorous situation from listening to "Polka.")

Second Lesson

At our last music listening lesson we heard part of a ballet called "The Age of Gold." What was the name of the part we heard? ("Polka") What is a ballet? (A story danced on the stage) What is a polka? (A dance in which couples step and hop around the room)

As you listened, you were supposed to picture dancers on a stage, but you discovered that the music had mechanical sounds that could make you think of machinery. It was music that could make you smile because, just as everything would seem to be going well, something would happen with a screech or a groan. Perhaps the dancers were showing off, trying to do tricky steps that were too difficult for them. There were many funny places.

As you listen to "Polka" today, raise your hands when you hear a place in the music that sounds funny to you.

(Play the record.)

Cat's Fugue (Intermediate)
Domenico Scarlatti
Italy, 1685–1757

Preparation for the Lessons

The music is in Musical Sound Books 78039.

First Lesson

The music we are to hear today, the "Cat's Fugue," was written by the Italian composer, Domenico Scarlatti, in the early 1700's. This was just before the piano was invented, and then, as now, the fugue was usually played on a harpsichord. Do you know anything about this instrument? (It has a keyboard like a piano, but inside, the strings are plucked by quills instead of being struck by felt hammers.)

The tune used in "Cat's Fugue" was supposedly created by a cat. There is a story that the composer, Scarlatti, had a large white cat, and one of his students had a little dog. One day when the dog was chasing the cat, it jumped upon the harpsichord keyboard to escape, and, as it walked, it accidentally played a tune which Scarlatti heard and wrote down to use as a theme for a fugue.

A fugue is a difficult piece of music to write because the beginning notes of the chief tune or theme must sound well when played with the last. In other words, the ending of the theme must be able to overlap the beginning. In this way, a fugue is like a round. Unlike a round, a fugue is always played on an instrument and never sung. Whereas the tune of a round always starts on the same note, the theme of a fugue is sometimes started from a low point on the keyboard, sometimes from a high, and sometimes from a place in between.

Probably Scarlatti made use of only a few notes which were "composed" by his cat and included in the fugue theme. These were at the beginning of the theme. They started low on the keyboard and progressed upward. The fast notes which followed and which rushed down the keyboard were probably added by Scarlatti to make the theme longer. As you listen to the recording of "Cat's Fugue," try to count how many times the theme starts. To be included in your count, a theme should have at least four notes which start low and move upward. Remember that the starting point will not be the same each time. Sometimes you will have to wait a while before you hear the theme again.

To help you start counting the entrances of the fugue theme, the first time it appears, I will hold up one finger, the second time two, the third time three fingers. Thereafter, count to yourselves.

(Play the record. The first playing of the theme will start with the first note, the second will start about five seconds later.)

How many times did you hear the cat's theme start? (Let several children answer. Eleven is a good guess, but any number between ten and thirteen is acceptable. The purpose of counting is not to find the exact number of times the theme begins but to help children become aware of the structure of the fugue.)

Second Lesson

At our last music listening lesson, we heard music whose main theme was supposedly composed by a cat. What was its name? ("Cat's Fugue") What did we find out about a fugue? (It has one important theme which is heard several times. The notes of the first part must sound well when they overlap the last. Unlike the tune of a round, the theme of a fugue can start on different pitches.)

Do you remember the name of the composer of "Cat's Fugue"? (Domenico Scarlatti) Scarlatti was born in Italy in 1685, the same year two other great composers, Johann Sebastian Bach and George Frederic Handel, were born in Germany. Scarlatti did not stay long in Italy. In those days musicians often worked for wealthy people or for royalty, and Scarlatti spent 25 years in Spain as composer and harpsichord player in the palace of the king and queen.

The harpsichord was one of the first keyboard instruments with strings on the inside which were played by pressing black and white keys with the fingers on the outside. It resembles the piano in appearance, but inside a piano, the strings are vibrated by little felt covered hammers, while inside a harpsichord, the strings are vibrated by quills which pluck them. When piano keys are pressed gently, the sound is soft; pressed forcefully, the sound is loud. Sounds from a harpsichord, however, all have the same intensity, and there can be no contrast between loud and soft. People who write music like to vary sound, and composers of harpsichord music had to find a way to manipulate the instrument. Can you guess what they did? (They probably had notes played singly for soft sounds and several notes played together to make a strong sound.)

Composers for harpsichord would keep the sound of their compositions varied and interesting by writing passages in which notes were sounded singly, and, when they wanted the music to build to a point of climax, a passage with many notes sounding simultaneously.

As you listen to "Cat's Fugue" today, try to find places of contrast in the music, and be ready to describe the elements the composer used to make the music varied and interesting.

(Play the record.)

How did Scarlatti bring contrast to the "Cat's Fugue" to hold his listeners' interest? (In some passages there were single notes playing, while in others, many notes were played simultaneously. There were contrasts in fast and slow passages.)

"Bourrée and Minuet II" from "Fireworks Music" (Intermediate)

George Frederic Handel
Germany, 1685–1759

Preparation for the Lessons

The music is in "Adventures in Music," Grade III, Volume 2; Musical Sound Books 78002; Bowmar Orchestral Library #62.

First Lesson

George Frederic Handel was born in Germany in 1685, the same year as two other famous musicians, Bach and Scarlatti. He was the son of a surgeon, or blood-letter, who was also a barber. As a young child, George showed great interest in toys that made musical sounds—toy trumpets, drums, whistles, flutes, and the like. His father was afraid that, as a result of this interest, his son might grow up to be a musician, and, since in those days, musicians were usually poor, Mr. Handel was determined that young George would do something else. He had all such toys hidden or thrown away. The child was not allowed to visit homes were there might be musical instruments or go to school where music was taught.

In spite of his father's attempts to stop him, George Frederic Handel continued to be interested in music. When he was seven, his aunt, who knew of his love for music, gave him a small-sized clavichord, an instrument something like a toy piano. This he smuggled into the attic where he played it in secret.

A short time later, George's father was called to the palace of the nearby duke. The boy knew that there were many clavichords in the palace, and he begged his father to allow him to go with him. Of course, his father refused, but young George persisted to the point of running after his father's carriage as it left for the palace. Finally, Mr. Handel relented and allowed the child to ride.

At the palace, George played the clavichords and the chapel organ. Everyone was amazed at his talent, and the Duke spoke strongly to the father, urging that the boy be given music lessons.

His father agreed, and thereafter George Handel studied harpsichord, violin, oboe, counterpoint, and composition with the church organist of his town. In three years he had done so well his teacher could teach him no more, and he was sent to the city of Berlin to study. There he met many famous musicians and also the king of Germany who offered to help pay for his musical education.

As luck would have it, Handel became a musician and was not poor at all. He was a church organist and choir director, and he wrote operas. He became so famous he was invited to go to England to give concerts on the organ and harpsichord and to direct his orchestral works. He enjoyed his visit to England and the life of London so much that he eventually returned to spend the last years of his life there.

It was while he lived in England that Handel composed the music we will hear today. The whole composition is titled "Fireworks Music" and was written in 1749 to celebrate the end of a very unpleasant war in Europe. The king of England decided there should be a day of festivities in a London park, including fireworks, an orchestra playing music by Handel, and a royal salute by over a hundred cannon.

The day of the celebration came. The orchestra played the introductory music, the cannon were shot off, and then, some of the fireworks displays accidentally caught fire and started going off in all directions. The park was soon a mass of flames and people rushing to get away. The evening was a failure, but Handel's music was not, for now, over 200 years later, people still listen to and enjoy his "Fireworks Music."

We will hear two parts of this music, "Bourrée" (boor-AY) and "Minuet II." These are the names of dances, and in the days of Handel, people enjoyed dance music so much, composers often wrote dances for people to sit and listen to. The "Fireworks Music" was just that, a set of dances to be heard rather than danced.

The "Bourrée" will be played first, and, as you listen to the music, you will notice that the tunes of the dance are repeated. Try to remember which group of instruments—stringed, woodwind, brass, or percussion—play the "Bourrée." Handel varies the repetition of the "Minuet" tunes by having different groups of instruments playing each repeat. Be able to tell which group plays the "Minuet" the first time, which the second, and which the third.

(Play the record.)

Which group of instruments played the "Bourrée"? (Stringed) Which played the "Minuet" the first time? (Stringed) The second? (Woodwind) The last time? (Brass with orchestra)

Second Lesson

Can you name the music which we heard at our last listening lesson? ("Bourrée" and "Minuet II" from the "Fireworks Music") What kind of music was this? (A set of dances) Who was the composer? (George Frederic Handel) About how long ago did he live? (Over 250 years ago)

A bourrée is a dance that was originally danced by wood cutters in wooden work shoes. It is said that they jumped in the air to click their heels together and then stamped their feet. These dance steps were repeated again and again, and Handel's tunes also are to be heard over and over.

There are two minuets in the "Fireworks Music," and the one we are hearing is the second. The minuet was popular when Washington was president and is a slower, more formal dance than the bourrée. When dancing it, partners stand straight, holding hands lightly. They take a few slow steps and then bow to each other. Again, there is repetition of steps, and again, Handel's music bears this out by repeating the tunes of the minuet.

At our last lesson we discovered what groups of instruments were used to play and repeat the tunes of the dances. We can guess that one reason composers have dance tunes played again is so that dancers can repeat the steps of a dance. Can you think of other reasons why composers would choose to have the tunes of any music repeated? (Let the children discuss this. Lead them to notice that people choose to repeat experiences that have given them pleasure; they might revisit places where they once enjoyed themselves or seek the company of people they have liked in the past.)

Human beings usually try to repeat anything that might once have given them pleasure. In the way that they repeat things is to be found the order or form, and in the way a composer has tunes appear and reappear can be found the pattern or form.

Today we will try to discover the form of the dances from Handel's "Fireworks Music." Both dances have two tunes. If we call the first tune of each dance "A" and the second one "B," we can make a picture of the pattern. Someone may write the patterns of the two dances on the chalk board as the music plays. (Choose a child or children to be at the board.) Those of you who are at your places may either write the pattern on a piece of paper or help the person(s) at the board by raising your hands briefly every time a tune begins. (Decide which procedure will be followed.)

(Play the record.)

The form of the "Bourrée" is: A A B B A A B B. The form of the "Minuet" is: A A B B A A B B A A B B. Why do you suppose Handel had different instrumental groups play the repeats of the "Minuet"? (To give contrast and variety and keep the listeners' interest)

"Romanze" from "Eine Kleine Nachtmusik" (Intermediate)
Wolfgang Amadeus Mozart
Austria, 1756–1791

Preparation for the Lessons

The music is in "Adventures in Music," Grade IV, Volume 1; Musical Sound Books 78004; Bowmar Orchestral Library #86.

First Lesson

The music we will hear today was written by the famous composer, Wolfgang Amadeus Mozart, who was born in Austria in 1756, a few years before America fought her war for independence.

Wolfgang Mozart had one of the most amazing childhoods of anyone who ever lived. When he was barely old enough to walk, he taught himself to play the harpsichord, a kind of old-fashioned piano. By the time he was four, he was composing minuets and had even written a concerto for orchestra. He also taught himself to play the violin at a very early age.

When he was only six, he and his talented older sister, Marianne, performed for the Empress of Austria. This event marked the beginning of a most unusual career. For a number of years thereafter, Wolfgang and his sister were taken by their father on a long concert tour of all the major cities of Europe.

Wolfgang was famous not only as a performer but also as a musical genius. People were continually testing his ability, asking him to do such things as play a harpsichord while its keys were covered with a cloth or read a difficult piece of music he had never seen before. In another test a musician would play a long and difficult piece, and the little boy would play it back, repeating it accurately. For all their hard work, the children were rewarded with lovely gifts, and Wolfgang was even given a diamond ring.

In those days travel by horse and carriage was very tiring, and the Mozart children were often sick. Wolfgang was continually composing as well as performing, and the combination of work and illness weakened him. As he grew older, other musicians showed their jealousy of him by preventing performances of his music. Because he could not earn money selling his compositions, he was very poor. However, he was not entirely unhappy, and the one great consolation of his short life was that he could constantly be writing music. He died a poor man at the age of 36, leaving behind him quantities of beautiful music.

What was Mozart's music like? One of his most famous compositions was a serenade called "Eine Kleine Nachtmusik," part of which we are to hear today. The idea of serenading people was started long ago by men who would go at night to the houses of the ladies they loved and sing under their windows. Later, serenade music was written for orchestras, and serenades were written to be played in honor of someone's birthday or some other event.

"Eine Kleine Nachtmusik" means "A Little Night Music" in English. It is a serenade in four parts, and we will be hearing the part called "Romanze," meaning "romance," a story of love and adventure. As you listen to the music, try to discover which group or groups of instruments—stringed, woodwind, brass, or percussion—are playing. Also, try to decide whether the music is formal or informal.

(Play the record.)

What group or groups of instruments did you hear in Mozart's "Romanze"? (Stringed) Did you feel that Mozart's music was formal or informal? (Formal) Why? (Every note could be heard clearly and the whole composition sounded carefully written.) What do we call the kind of music that is written to be played under someone's window at night? (A serenade)

Second Lesson

At our last music listening lesson, we heard a part of "Eine Kleine Nachtmusik," music originally written to be played under someone's window at night. What is it called? (A serenade) Who wrote the music? (Wolfgang Amadeus Mozart) What was the name of the part we heard?

("Romanze") Did it sound formal or informal? (Formal—the notes sounded carefully written.)

Mozart lived at around the time Washington was president. Not only was music formal in style in those days; people were formal and restrained in other areas. Can you think of other ways in which people expressed formality in their living? (People were formal in the way they dressed, in their manners, and in their dancing. Their clothing was restricting; art and architecture were carefully designed, etc.)

People in Mozart's time lived by rules. There were even rules for planning music and giving it a pattern or form. The form Mozart used in "Romanze" was called the rondo. Rondo is an Italian word that sounds a little like the word "round" in English. In a sense, the music of a rondo does go 'round and 'round, in that it always returns to the first tune. If we call the first tune of a rondo "A" and the second tune "B," and so forth, we find that the form or pattern of a rondo is A B A C A D A for as far as the composer wishes to go.

As you listen to Mozart's "Romanze" today, try to hear the return of the "A" tune. It will be repeated at least once before each alternate tune is heard. Raise your hand every time you hear the "A" tune return. If possible, try to remember how many different tunes were used.

(Play the record. The children should raise their hands for the start of the "A" tune like this: A A (interlude) A B B A A C C A A (interlude) A-type coda.)

Were you able to hear how many different tunes Mozart used? (There were three major tunes, an interlude, and a coda or ending.) If the tunes of this music were charted without repeats, the pattern would look like this: A B A C A Coda. What is the name of thi form? (Rondo)

"Allegretto" from "Symphony No. 8" (Intermediate)
Ludwig van Beethoven
Germany, 1770–1827

Preparation for the Lessons

The music is in "Adevntures in Music," Grade IV, Volume 1; Bowmar Orchestral Library #71.

First Lesson

Today we will be hearing music which was written by Ludwig van Beethoven (BAY-tow-ven), a composer who is considered to have been one of the greatest who ever lived.

Ludwig van Beethoven was born in Germany in 1770 near the time of the American revolution. He was the son of a not-too-successful musician, and, when Ludwig showed musical talent as a child, his father hoped he might become another child prodigy like Mozart, who just a few years previously, at the age of six, had become famous for the concerts he gave in the capitol cities of Europe. With this in mind, the boy was forced to practice the harpsichord, a kind of old-fashioned piano, for hours every day. When he made a mistake, his father would become badly upset and beat him or box his ears.

After Ludwig's mother died, his father worsened and became increasingly difficult until, when Ludwig was seventeen, the courts appointed him guardian of his two younger brothers. Thereafter he worked in earnest to support the family.

You can imagine how such a childhood affected Beethoven when he grew up. As an adult he had no patience and was irritable even with his best friends. When he was in his late twenties, he started to lose his hearing, and this depressed him to the point where he sometimes felt it was useless to go on living if he could not hear his own music. During the last years of his life, he was quite deaf and could only "hear" his music in his imagination.

Composing music did not come easy for Beethoven. He would make a first draft of a composition, revise it, and write it again and again until it satisfied him. Seldom did he compose quickly, but the music we are to hear today happens to be an exception. He wrote his "Eighth Symphony" in a relatively short period of time, and we will be listening to part of it.

A symphony is a long piece of music written to be played by a symphony orchestra of about 100 players. When the form of the symphony was being worked out some 200 years ago, composers realized that audiences might become tired or lose interest in such a long piece. Therefore, they divided it into three or four sections or shorter pieces called movements. The first movement was to be rather fast, the second slow, the third gay and medium fast, and the fourth very fast and exciting. By having each movement at a different speed, listeners were kept interested.

Today we will listen to the second movement of Beethoven's "Symphony No. 8," marked "Allegretto." This is an Italian music word which tells the orchestra that the music should be played "not too fast." As you listen, try to hear the group or groups of instruments Beethoven chose, and decide if they are stringed, woodwind, brass, or percussion. Also listen for sounds in the music which you think reveal the sensitive feelings, restlessness, and impatience in Beethoven's personality.

(Play the record.)

What groups of instruments did Beethoven use in the "Allegretto" of his "Eighth Symphony"? (Stringed and woodwind) Beethoven chose not to use the stronger sounds of brass and percussion.

What sounds did you hear in the music which reflected Beethoven's personality? (Encourage the children to discuss the character of the music. Help them to remember the sounds of seeming impatience in the sudden loud places and equally sudden softenings, the quick changes from high sounds to low and back to high again, etc.) Beethoven might have the highest instruments play a phrase as if they were asking a question; then he would have the lowest instruments play an answer. Or, after having the orchestra make "tiptoeing" sounds, he might have it suddenly play very loudly.

Second Lesson

The "Allegretto" from "Symphony No. 8" which we heard at our last lesson was written by Ludwig van Beethoven after he became deaf. He could only imagine the sounds of the notes in his head and plan what form the second movement would take without ever hearing it.

In planning for the "Allegretto," Beethoven decided that he would have the first melody, or theme, repeated, and, to make it more interesting, have it played with slight changes or variations each time. This is called "developing" a theme, having it played in variation. If you were a music writer, could you think of ways to vary a tune? (Let the children think of possibilities—have different instruments play it, change the accompaniment, have it played soft and loud, have it played high one time, low the next, etc.)

In writing the "Allegretto," Beethoven had to find a theme which would sound well when it was developed or played in various ways. He probably experimented with several tunes before he found one that suited him. As you listen to it today, you will notice that the theme he chose is only a few measures long. Try to hear every variation and be prepared to describe each in words.

The music begins with seven chords, quickly played. Raise your hand immediately after this short introduction, which is when the theme is first heard. Lower your hand and wait until each time it starts again.

(Play the record. The children should raise their hands after the seven-chord introduction and soon thereafter when the theme is played in a slightly lower key. After an interlude, the theme returns. When it is repeated, it is played with extra notes. It never returns, and the music ends rather abruptly.)

What is meant by "development of a theme"? (The repetition of a tune in various ways) How did Beethoven develop the theme in the "Allegretto" of his "Eighth Symphony"? (He had it played in a lower key, and he had it played with extra notes to make it sound louder and brighter.)

"Scherzo" from "A Midsummer Night's Dream" (Intermediate)

Felix Mendelssohn
Germany, 1809–1847

Preparation for the Lessons

The music is in Musical Sound Books #78026; Bowmar Orchestral Library #57. The play, *A Midsummer Night's Dream*, is by William Shakespeare.

First Lesson

The music we are to hear today is called "Scherzo" (SKER-tso). It is one of a set of pieces written to be played between the acts of *A Midsummer Night's Dream*, a play by William Shakespeare. The composer is Felix Mendelssohn, and the "Scherzo" is played just before Act Two.

Scherzo is an Italian word meaning "joke," and a joke is exactly what is being undertaken in Shakespeare's play. The king and the queen of fairies, Oberon and Titania, are in a forest with their subjects and attendants. They are arguing and quarreling because the fairy queen is giving her attentions to a young boy and her husband is jealous.

Titania leaves the scene, and Oberon calls Puck, the elf whose job it is to entertain the king by doing mischief. The fairy king sends Puck to get a magic herb whose juice, when squeezed on the eyelids of a sleeping person, will put him under a spell and make him think he loves the first person he sees when he awakes. After Puck delivers it to him, Oberon drops the herb juice on the eyelids of the sleeping Titania.

You can imagine the confusion when the fairy queen wakes up! The first creature she sees is a man in a donkey's head, a workman who happens to be in the forest rehearsing a play. Titania immediately thinks she loves him, and she has her fairy attendants cover his neck with wreaths of flowers. But, that is getting ahead of the story because that incident is in the next act of the play, and the "Scherzo" is only supposed to describe the scene in the second act when the mischief is being done.

As you listen to Mendelssohn's music, try to discover passages in the music that have sounds which remind you of the characters in the play and that help you picture the action that is taking place.

(Play the record.)

What sounds did you hear in the music to remind you of the characters and of the action in Act Two of *A Midsummer Night's Dream*? (You could hear the sounds of fairies flitting through the forest, of Titania and Oberon arguing, of Puck tiptoeing about playing tricks, of the queen asleep, etc.)

Second Lesson

What was the name of the play by Shakespeare for which we heard music at our last listening lesson? (*A Midsummer Night's Dream*) Who composed the music? (Felix Mendelssohn)

Felix Mendelssohn was born in Germany in 1809, the same year that Abraham Lincoln was born in a log cabin in the United States. The Mendelssohn family was very wealthy, and for most of Felix's childhood, they lived in a large mansion in the midst of spacious lawns and lovely gardens. On one part of the estate was a private park with large old trees and, in the garden, a large garden house with a concert hall which could hold over 100 people. During the week, the four Mendelssohn children played in the house, and on many weekends, they would give concerts for their friends.

These concerts were popular and pleasant affairs. Felix had started writing music for the piano at an early age, and he and his sister Fanny would play his compositions. When he wanted to hear the music he had written for orchestra, his wealthy father would hire a group of musicians to play it. Since the child was too small to be seen by the players, he had to stand on a chair to conduct them.

In spite of family wealth, none of the Mendelssohn children were spoiled. They were expected to practice their music every day but Sunday, starting as early as five in the morning. But, they enjoyed this kind of work and were always happy.

Most of Mendelssohn's compositions reflect the happiness of his life. He traveled a great deal to introduce his music. He would perform his piano compositions and conduct his orchestral works in the capitols of Europe. Everywhere, the people loved him.

Mendelssohn read Shakespeare's plays when he was a young boy, and he found the story of *A Midsummer Night's Dream* very amusing. He started composing music based on the plot when he was just 17. When he grew up, the king of Germany requested that he write incidental music for between the acts of the play, and it was then that the "Scherzo" or joke music was written.

The music describes the characters and action which is to take place in Act Two—the fairies flitting about, king Oberon and queen Titania arguing, the elf, Puck, tiptoeing about, the queen sleeping. But music, unlike words in a story, need not describe events in order. In the "Scherzo," for instance, the "fairy music" returns again and again, although in the play the fairies do not reappear repeatedly or in this particular order.

As you listen to the "Scherzo" today, see how well you recognize the "fairy music," and raise your hands every time you hear it. This will give you a picture of the pattern Mendelssohn followed when he was composing this music.

(Play the record. The children should raise their hands twice in the beginning, once in the middle, and once after a long, rising scale passage. At the very end, they should raise their hands once more when the flutes start to play.)

Claire de Lune (Intermediate)
Claude Debussy
France, 1862–1918

Preparation for the Lessons

The music is in RCA Victor "Listening Activities," Volume V; Musical Sound Books #78153; Bowmar Orchestral Library #52. If possible, have available pictures by Impressionist painters like Renoir, Van Gogh, Cezanne, Monet, Seurat, etc.

First Lesson

——————————————

The music we are to hear today is called "Clair de Lune," French words meaning "light of the moon" or "moonlight." It was written by the composer, Claude Debussy (de-boo-SEE), who was born in France in 1862.

At the same time Debussy was writing music in the last part of the 19th century, a group of artists was experimenting with new ways of painting pictures. Instead of making paintings which resembled photographs, they were using colors and lines which merely gave the viewer an impression of the thing being pictured. These artists were called Impressionists because their pictures suggested the subject matter without giving much detail. (Show pictures by Impressionist painters if available.)

As an example of this kind of art, let us suppose an Impressionist were painting grass in a scene. Most likely he would put small amounts of colors like pink, yellow, purple, and blue, as well as shades of green, because these might have been the first colors he thought he saw when he looked quickly at the actual grass. Of course, these are colors everyone sees when the sun shines on grass that is wet with dew. This is how we get an impression of grass from these dabs of various colors in the Impressionist's painting.

Just as these artists were experimenting with painting, so was Claude Debussy experimenting with creating vague-sounding music that merely gave the listener a hazy impression of what he should envision. He was called an Impressionist composer, and "Clair de Lune" is a good example of this rather vague and indistinct type of music. Debussy never told us exactly what scene to picture, and everyone is welcome to imagine whatever strikes his fancy. As you listen, it will be better if you picture moonlight falling on something rather than continually picturing the moon in the sky. Imagine how an object or a beautiful scene would look with moonlight resting upon it.

(Play the record.)

As you listened to "Claire de Lune," what did you picture? (Let the children describe what they envisioned as they listened.)

Second Lesson

At our last listening lesson, we heard music by a French composer who experimented with sound in the late 19th and early 20th centuries. What was his name? (Claude Debussy) What was his style of composing? (Impressionistic) What was the name of the composition we heard? ("Claire de Lune") What does this mean in English? (Moonlight)

All music is necessarily indefinite. It is impossible to create music which will in every respect remind listeners of one particular scene or of an exact picture. The sounds of Impressionistic music are especially vague, and yet, as you listened to "Claire de Lune" in the previous lesson, there were elements in the music that helped you imagine a scene touched by moonlight.

We know that Impressionist artists used various techniques to give impressions. Among them were such methods as dabbing spots of paint on canvas and applying touches of color that appeared strange when seen close up. Debussy had compositional techniques which he used to enable his listeners to get impressions. As you listen to "Claire de Lune" today, try to discover what those techniques are.

(Play the record.)

What were some of the compositional techniques which Debussy used in his impressionistic music? (Children might observe that: melodies were not strong or important-sounding, notes seemed to merge with one another, chords were held and allowed to run over into others, there was a rolling sound in much of the accompaniment, the harmony was modern with notes close together, there were no heavy chords, sudden loud sounds, or harsh accents.)

"Hoe-Down" from "Rodeo" (Intermediate)
Aaron Copland
U.S.A., 1900–

Preparation for the Lessons

The music is in "Adventures in Music," Grade V, Volume 2; Bowmar Orchestral Library #55.

First Lesson

Dancing is an ancient form of human expression. In ballroom dancing or folk dancing, almost everyone can participate. But there are more difficult dances which can only be performed by people who have been trained and rehearsed, and the ballet which is danced on a stage is one of the oldest of this type.

In thinking of ballet, most of us think of the Russian style in which the ladies wear short, full skirts, and everyone wears special shoes so they can twirl rapidly on their toes. The ballet might tell a story, or the performers might interpret the music. In modern ballet, too, the dancers wear toe shoes, but the costumes they wear are usually regular clothing that will go with the story.

Today we are going to hear part of the music for a modern ballet called "Rodeo," written by the American composer, Aaron Copland. Mr. Copland was born in Brooklyn, New York, in 1900. His father was the owner of a department store where Aaron often worked during his high school years. The money he earned went for music lessons. He saved enough to take him to France where he continued his studies. He is one of America's foremost composers, and is famous not only for the music he has written, but also because he is an author and lecturer on the art of enjoying and understanding music.

The rodeo is a well-known part of American life. In what part of the country would you expect to find rodeos? (The west) What are some of the events which take place at a rodeo? (Riding broncos, roping and tying cattle, rounding up livestock, etc.)

The story in the ballet, "Rodeo," centers around a young girl in her teens. She appears at the rodeo in pigtails and blue jeans, and everyone treats her like a child. She is showing off until she is thrown by a bronco, and this makes everyone laugh.

In the next scene everyone is at the Saturday night dance, and only the young cowgirl is not having fun. She leaves abruptly, and the dancing continues in high spirits. The hoe-down, a kind of square dance, starts, and this is the part of the music we shall hear.

The stage is full of happy people in colorful square dance costumes. The "Hoe-down" music begins with the fiddler tuning up. You can imagine couples getting into position. The caller starts calling the steps, and everyone starts to clap and dance.

Suddenly, something happens. The music slows, and the dancing stops. Can you guess why? (Give the children a chance to guess.) Everyone has stopped to look at a figure standing in the doorway. It is the young cowgirl who has transformed herself into a beautiful young lady. Her hair is long and held by a bow, and she is wearing a dress. The young men rush up to ask her to dance, but she refuses them—all but the roper, the only one who had befriended her.

The music starts over with more spirit than ever. Toes tap and hands clap; everyone circles left and right; partners swing wildly on skipping feet; they twine around each other in a grand right and left. Try to picture the action as you listen to "Hoe-down."

(Play the record.)

What did the "Hoe-down" music help you picture? (The children should remark about the sounds of the fiddle tuning, square dance music, the pause as everyone looks at the girl in the doorway, the whirling, toe-tapping, hand-clapping dancers, and so forth.)

Second Lesson

What was the music we heard at our last listening lesson? ("Hoe-down" from "Rodeo") Who was the composer? (Aaron Copland) For what kind of stage performance was this music? (Ballet)

Mr. Copland's "Hoe-down" music was written to be danced. The story which the ballet dancers tell on the stage has humor, merriment, and playfulness, and a happy ending for the once-awkward cowgirl. The instruments which were chosen helped keep the mood of gaiety and good fun as well as the spirit of dancing. Notice the orchestration as you listen to "Hoe-down" today, and try to remember which instruments helped the dancing and which helped express humor. If there are too many to remember, list them on paper.

(Play the record.)

What instruments were used to make people feel like dancing? (Violins and strings, trumpets and brasses, oboe and clarinet were the predominating instruments used to inspire dancing.) What instruments were used to show humor? (Wood block, piano, 'cellos and double basses were used to create a humorous effect. Xylophone, drum, tuba, trombone, and cymbals were used less obviously.)

Third Lesson

The first time we listened to "Hoe-down" by Aaron Copland, we pictured the story that was danced on the ballet stage. The second time we heard it, we discovered how Mr. Copland used instruments to inspire dancing and to express a mood of humor.

As we listen to "Hoe-down" today, we will look for pattern in the music. Pattern or form is revealed in tunes that are repeated. In actual square dancing, a single tune will often be played again and again while dancers do different steps and patterns.

To find the pattern in the music, you will listen for an old square dance tune which Mr. Copland has the orchestra play five times. First you will hear the fiddles tune up; piano, wood block, and basses will play a humorous boogie-woogie type passage; and then the tune will appear, played by violins and hardly noticeable. Raise your hands when it starts. Listen carefully, and you will hear it twice again. Then a solo trumpet plays a second tune, and a third tune something like "Turkey in the Straw" comes in. Keep listening. After the music pauses and moves slowly, the tune will return twice again. Raise your hands each time it starts.

———————

(Play the record. The children will raise their hands three times in the beginning and twice after the slow interlude.)

A Final Word from the Author

This book has been written to help give teachers confidence in their own ability to present music lessons. The teacher who is sure of himself will not only enjoy teaching music but will see his feelings of interest and enthusiasm reflected in his pupils.

Music is gratifying and pleasurable, but, is it important, you may ask. We know that reading is important. We need mathematics, and science has value. But do we need music? Music does not help us in our living in any conspicuous way—does not help feed us, clothe or shelter us. It does not keep us from harm; it does not add to our wealth. It is nothing more than an intangible which passes quickly. Yet, man continually chooses to create and re-create it through the years. What is its attraction?

Music affects us at a subconscious level. It is one of the means by which man shows his need to perceive and deal with certain aspects of life symbolically. In the dreams of his sleep, his subconscious mind resolves emotional dilemmas, alleviates anxieties, crystallizes attitudes, under the subterfuge of symbols. When he creates his arts and his music, man openly expresses his interest in and ability to treat life symbolically. The organized sounds that are music reassure him and help him feel a sense of his own dignity and of the values of all life.

The arts and music will be needed more than ever in the near future when people live in a world of extended leisure time. Present-day schools which are preparing children to be citizens of tomorrow must provide for them experiences with subjects which have lasting and intrinsic value. These would include exposure to great literature, great art, and great music. They would also include opportunities to write, to paint and draw, and to sing and move to music.

BIBLIOGRAPHY

Balet, Jan, *What Makes an Orchestra*. New York, N.Y.: Oxford University Press, 1951. The text tells about the instruments and the conductor of the orchestra and is cleverly illustrated by the author.

Commins, Dorothy B., *All About the Symphony Orchestra and What It Plays*. New York, N. Y.: Random House, Inc., 1961. The illustrations show people playing the various instruments.

Kettlekamp, Larry, *Drums, Rattles and Bells*. New York, N.Y.: William Morrow and Company, Inc., 1960. Gives a history of the instruments and explains how to make and play them. For grades 3–6.

Kettlekamp, Larry, *Flutes, Whistles and Reeds*. New York, N.Y.: William Morrow and Company, Inc., 1962. See above.

Kettlekamp, Larry, *Horns*. New York, N. Y.: William Morrow and Company, Inc., 1964. See above.

Kettlekamp, Larry, *Singing Strings*. New York, N. Y.: William Morrow and Company, Inc., 1958. See above.

Mirsky, Reba Paeff, *Beethoven*. Chicago, Illinois: Follett Publishing Company, 1957. Stories about events in the life of the composer for children at the intermediate level.

Mirsky, Reba Paeff, *Johann Sebastian Bach*. Chicago, Illinois: Follett Publishing Company, 1965. See above.

Mirsky, Reba Paeff, *Mozart*. Chicago, Illinois: Follett Publishing Company, 1960. See above.

Posell, Elsa Z., *This Is an Orchestra*. Boston, Mass.: Houghton Mifflin Company, 1950. Illustrated with clearcut photographs of the instruments. For grades 4–6.

Suggs, William W., *Meet the Orchestra*. New York, N. Y.: The Macmillan

Company, 1966. An informative book illustrated with drawings of the instruments in the various sections of the orchestra. For grades 3–6.

Wheeler, Opal, *Handel at the Court of Kings*. New York, N. Y.: E. P. Dutton & Company, Inc., 1943. Stories about the composer as a child for children in grades 3–6.

Wheeler, Opal, *Ludwig Beethoven and the Chiming Bells*. New York, N. Y.: E. P. Dutton & Company, Inc. See above.

Wheeler, Opal, and Sybil Deutcher, *Mozart the Wonder Boy*. New York, N. Y.: E. P. Dutton & Company, Inc., 1934. See above.

Wheeler, Opal, and Sybil Deutcher, *Sebastian Bach, the Boy from Thuringia*. New York, N. Y.: E. P. Dutton & Company, Inc., 1937. See above.

SOURCE MATERIALS FOR MUSIC LESSONS

Following are names and addresses of companies which can supply materials for music lessons:

Basic Music Texts for Grades 1–6

Birchard Music Series, 1958–1962
    Summy-Birchard Company
    1834 Ridge Avenue
    Evanston, Illinois 60204

Discovering Music Together, 1966
    Follett Publishing Company
    1010 West Washington Boulevard
    Chicago, Illinois 60607

Exploring Music, 1966
    Holt, Rinehart and Winston, Inc.
    383 Madison Avenue
    New York, N.Y. 10017

Growing with Music, 2nd Edition, 1966
    Prentice-Hall, Inc.
    Englewood Cliffs, New Jersey 07632

The Magic of Music, 1965–1968
    Ginn and Company
    72 Fifth Avenue
    New York, N. Y. 10011

Making Music Your Own, 1964
    Silver Burdett Company
    Box 362
    Morristown, New Jersey 07960

Music for Young Americans, 2nd Edition, 1966
    American Book Company
    300 Pike Street
    Cincinnati, Ohio 45202

This Is Music, 2nd Edition, 1967–1968
    Allyn and Bacon, Inc.
    470 Atlantic Avenue
    Boston, Mass. 02210

Catalog Sources for Autoharps

1. National Autoharp Sales Co.
   P. O. Box 1120
   Des Moines, Iowa 50311

2. Oscar Schmidt-International, Inc.
   87 Ferry Street
   Jersey City, New Jersey 07307

3. Walberg and Ange
   86 Mechanic Street
   Worcester, Massachusetts

Catalog Sources for Pictures of Composers, Instruments

1. Keyboard, Jr.
   1346 Chapel Street
   New Haven, Connecticut 06511

2. Lyons
   223 West Lake Street
   Chicago, Illinois 60606

Catalog Sources for Pitchpipes

1. Willam Kratt Company
   988 Johnson Place
   Union, New Jersey

2. Lyons
   223 West Lake Street
   Chicago, Illinois 60606

Catalog Sources for Records

"Adventures in Music" (ten volumes)
RCA Victor "Listening Activities" (six volumes)
RCA Victor "Rhythmic Activities" (six volumes)

All of the above albums are available from:
    RCA Victor Educational Sales

155 East 24th Street
New York, N. Y. 10010

"Bowmar Orchestral Library" is available from:
Bowmar Records
10515 Burbank Boulevard
North Hollywood, California 91601

"Musical Sound Books" are available from:
Sound Books Press Society, Inc.
Scarsdale, New York

Catalog Sources for Record Players

1. Califone Corporation
   1041 North Sycamore Street
   Hollywood, California

2. Newcomb Audio Products Co.
   6824 Lexington Avenue
   Hollywood, California 90038

3. Webster Chicago Corporation (WEBCOR)
   5601 West Bloomingdale Avenue
   Chicago, Illinois 60639

Catalog Sources for Miscellaneous Supplies

1. Children's Music Center, Inc. (for records, books)
   5373 West Pico Boulevard
   Los Angeles, California 90019

2. Educational Record Sales (for records)
   157 Chambers Street
   New York, N. Y. 10007

3. Lyons (for Autoharps, books, pictures, pitchpipes, records, record
   players, staff liners, etc.)
   223 West Lake Street
   Chicago, Illinois 60606

INDEX

INDEX

A

"Ach, Ja!" (German folk dance), 55-6
"Allegretto" from "Symphony No. 8," 181-4
Autoharp, how to play, 114-16

B

Bach, Johann Sebastian, 163-5
"Badinerie" from "Suite in B Minor," 163-5
Basic rhythms, how to teach, 23-4
Beachball activities (rhythm lessons), 38-9
Beethoven, Ludvig van, 181-4
"Black-Eyed Susie" (square dance music), 73-5
"Bluebird, Bluebird" (Texas singing game) , 44-6
"Bourrée and Minuet II" from "Fireworks Music," 176-9
Brass instruments, 152-4

C

"Cat's Fugue," 174-6
"Children's Symphony," 1st and 3rd movements, 170-3
"Chimes of Dunkirk" (French folk dance), 51-2
Chords, constructing, 112-13
"Christmas Dance" (Swedish folk dance), 54-5

"Claire de Lune," 186-7
Clapping (rhythm lessons), 24-6
Composer, learning about, 158-9
Copland, Aaron, 187-90
"Crested Hen, The" (Danish folk dance), 62-4
"Cshebogar" (Hungarian folk dance), 61-2

D

Dance suite, 161-2
Debussy, Claude, 167-8, 186-7
Descriptive music, 159-60
Dramatizing songs, 85

E

Eighth notes (reading lesson), 94
"Entrance of the Little Fauns," 168-9
Exposing children to music, 137-8

F

Folk dances and singing games:
  American,
    Black-Eyed Susie (square dance), 73-5
    Bluebird, Bluebird, 44-6
    Maypole Streamer Dance, 47-9
    Old Brass Wagon, 50-51
    Pop! Goes the Weasel, 59-61
    Shoo, Fly, Don't Bother Me, 49-50
    Turkey in the Straw (Virginia reel), 68-70

Pitchpipe, use of, 79-80
"Polka" (Czechoslovakian folk dance), 66-8
"Polka" from "The Age of Gold," 173-4
"Pop! Goes the Weasel" (American folk dance), 59-61

Q

Quarter notes and rests (reading lessons), 92-4

R

Records, teaching songs with, 85
Repeated notes (reading lessons), 100-102
Responding to music, 162
Rhythm, feeling and hearing differences in, 89-91
Rhythm, notation of, 91-2, 110
Rhythms, how to teach basic, 23-4
"Romanze" from "Eine Kleine Nachtmusik," 179-81
Rote, teaching a song by, 82, 84
Running (rhythm lesson), 33-4

S

Scale in music (reading lessons), 97-100
Scarlatti, Domenico, 174-6
"Scherzo" from "A Midsummer Night's Dream," 184-6
"Shoo, Fly, Don't Bother Me" (American singing game), 49-50
Shostakovitch, Dmitri, 173-4
Singing games, see Folk dances
Singing, how to teach, 77-86
Skating (rhythm lesson), 34-5
Skipping (rhythm lessons), 30-32
Songs:
  accompanied by one chord,
    Are You Sleeping? 116
    Frère Jacques, 116
    Lone Star Trail, The, 117
    Lovely Evening, 117
    Ring Around a Rosy, 116
    Row, Row, Row Your Boat, 116
    Taps, 117
  accompanied by two chords,
    Clementine, 124-5
    Did You Ever See a Lassie? 118-19
    Down by the Station, 120
    Down in the Valley, 122
    Eency Weency Spider, 118

Songs: (cont.)
  accompanied by two chords, (cont.)
    Farmer in the Dell, The, 117
    Go Tell Aunt Rhodie, 120-21
    He's Got the Whole World in His Hands, 123
    Hot Cross Buns, 120
    Hush, Little Baby, 121
    John Brown Had a Little Indian, 119
    Joshua Fit the Battle of Jericho, 124
    Leavin' Old Texas, 123-4
    London Bridge, 117-18
    Long, Long Ago, 124
    Mary Had a Little Lamb, 118
    More We Get Together, The, 121
    Mulberry Bush, 118
    Pawpaw Patch, 119-20
    Polly Wolly Doodle, 121-2
    Rig-a-Jig-Jig, 123
    Three Blind Mice, 120
    Where Has My Little Dog Gone? 119
  accompanied by three chords,
    America, 129
    Auld Lang Syne, 133
    Away in a Manger, 131-2
    Bingo, 127
    Camptown Races, 132
    For He's a Jolly Good Fellow, 130
    Go Tell it on the Mountain, 134
    Hickory Dickory Dock, 125-6
    Home on the Range, 133-4
    I'm a Little Teapot, 125
    Jingle Bells, 132
    Lavender's Blue, 130
    Man on the Flying Trapeze, 129
    Muffin Man, The, 125
    My Country 'Tis of Thee, 129
    Oats and Beans and Barley Grow, 127
    O Christmas Tree, 131
    Oh, Susanna, 130
    Old MacDonald Had a Farm, 126
    Red River Valley, 135
    She'll Be Comin' 'Round the Mountain, 128
    Silent Night, 131
    Swanee River, 132-3
    Swing Low, Sweet Chariot, 134
    This Old Man, 127-8
    Twinkle, Twinkle, Little Star, 126
    Up on the House-Top, 126
    Yankee Doodle, 128-9
Square dance directions, 74-5
Stringed instruments, 149-52
Symphony, form of, 171-3, 182-4